THE CEO OF ME

Because Your Health Is Your Business

ADRIAN M. WILLIAMS

Cybersecurity Leader | Executive Health Strategist | Certified Personal Trainer

To my father —

*whose story taught me that the most important signal
is the one you act on early.*

And to every leader who decides their health

is worth governing with the same intention

they bring to everything else.

ACKNOWLEDGMENTS

There are books that come from research. This one came from people.

Mom

Everything I know about showing up starts with you. You supported every sport, every dream, every direction I decided to point myself — not because you had to, but because that is who you are. You gave me unconditional love and the discipline to do something with it. I did not always appreciate the discipline in the moment. I appreciate it now more than you know. This book exists because you raised someone who refused to quit. That is your work as much as mine.

My Sister and Brother

You have never judged me. Not once. You love me for exactly who I am — the quirks, the intensity, the habits that make other people raise an eyebrow. The inside jokes that only make sense to us. The moments we just look at each other and move on without a word. That kind of love does not need explaining. I am grateful for it every day.

My Kids

I could not have asked for better. Not even close. Watching you grow into the people you have become is something I do not have the right words for. You are adults now building your own lives — and every day you show me that the lesson was passed down. Your healthy habits, the way you carry yourselves, the fact that you have a system to bring you back when life pulls you off track — that is not an accident. That is everything I hoped for.

But what moves me most is watching you bet on yourselves. The entrepreneurial spirit you carry, the way you have figured out how to use every tool available to you — including platforms and spaces that did not even exist when I was your age — to build something that is entirely your own. You did not wait for a path to appear. You made one. And you had the courage to take chances most people only talk about.

I cannot express how proud I am. Not just of what you have built — but of who you are while you are building it. The legacy I talk about in this book is not abstract to me. It has your faces on it. You are the reason the standard matters. You always have been.

Family and Friends

To the rest of my family and friends — thank you for the love, the support, and the patience. Particularly the patience. I know I come with some very specific conditions. My food cannot touch. I do not eat leftovers. I only eat certain things from certain people. I have a few rules. You have never made me feel strange for any of it. You just adjust, shake your head slightly, and keep going. That is love. Thank you for it.

My Clients and the 5 a.m. Crew

Over thirty years ago I started showing up before the day started. That home gym — the first of three — is where the foundation of this book was built, one early morning at a time. About four years in, Delvin joined me, and he has been the most consistent presence ever since. Some people talk about accountability. Delvin lives it. More than twenty-five years of showing up, no excuses, no drama. That means more than I can say.

But it was never just the two of us. Over the years, hundreds of people came through — family, friends, friends of friends, strangers who showed up one morning because they needed a change and stayed because they found something real. Three home gyms later, I want every one of you to know: the lessons in this book came through those doors. You held me accountable every single day — not by saying anything, but by showing up. You taught me more about consistency, about human nature, and about what people are truly capable of when the environment is right than any certification ever could. I am grateful for every one of you. You built this book with me without knowing it.

Tasha

And to my wife Tasha — where do I even begin.

You are the reason this book exists. Not because you pushed me to write it — but because of who you are and what you bring out in me every day. You make me want to be better — as a husband, as a father, as a man.

You are my peace in a life that moves fast, and my anchor when it moves too fast.

In this book I talk about the importance of a Health Board — and specifically the Chair. The person who tells you the truth when comfort is easier. The person who holds the standard when you want to negotiate with it. The person whose long-term investment in your health is greater than anyone else's because they are building a life with you. That is you. It has always been you.

But more than that — you are my partner in every real sense of the word. You did not just support this journey. You took it with me. Every standard I kept, you kept yours. Every early morning I committed to, you held your own standard beside me. That is not support. That is partnership. And it makes all the difference.

We have talked about our 90s more times than most couples talk about next year. Not what we will have accumulated — but what we will still be able to do. Still moving. Still sharp. Still choosing each other on purpose. That shared vision is not just something we talk about — it is the standard we govern by. Every decision in this book, I made with that picture in mind. With you in it.

Without you, I am not the man I am today. You are my motivation to be better. You are my peace. This book is truly dedicated to you. Everything I do is for us. And when we are in our 90s — still moving, maybe not as fast, but moving — the principles in this book will have proven what we both believed: that it was worth it. All of it. Every early morning. Every standard we refused to compromise. Every decision we made to take care of ourselves so we could take care of each other.

I love you.

God willing, we will still be doing exactly this — together.

TABLE OF CONTENTS

Each chapter includes:

Named Framework · Action Steps · Executive Debrief · Operating Sheets

THE CEO OF ME

Because Your Health Is Your Business

Adrian M. Williams

Before We Begin

There are moments when theory stops being theoretical.

For me, that moment came with a phone call from my sister.

She told me our dad had found a lump behind his ear. He had already decided what it was. He told her he thought it was cancer. He told her he was going to die.

Now, if you know anything about men—especially our fathers' generation—you know how rare that kind of vulnerability is; most of us are stubborn. They avoided doctors like an audit. No pain, no problem. If it doesn't hurt, it doesn't exist. Until the bill comes due.

My dad and I both lived by that rule. Annual physicals felt optional. Preventive screenings were for other people. If nothing was obviously wrong, you kept moving.

So when my sister called, part of me assumed she was overreacting.

My mother, who is a nurse, joined the call. Calm but firm, she said what medical professionals always say in these moments: get it checked. It could be something, or it could be nothing. But you will not know unless you go.

We pushed. For months.

And like a lot of men, my dad brushed it off. "I'm fine. It'll go away. I don't need a doctor."

Until my sister stopped asking and took action. She got him in the car and drove him to the hospital herself.

He was right.

It was cancer. Rare. Aggressive. He was referred to Johns Hopkins—one of the best cancer centers in the country. Things moved quickly. The treatment plan was radical. Surgeons removed the tumor, including part of his face.

It was traumatic. But it worked.

Until it didn't.

Once the crisis passed, my dad slipped back into the same avoidance. The same habits. Follow-ups became inconsistent. Prevention faded. Life resumed.

The cancer came back. This time, the margin was gone.

We lost him.

That experience left me with a truth I carry into every conversation in this book: most people don't fail because they don't care. They fail because they delay leadership. And delay always has a price.

That delayed cost has a name: the Pain Tax.

That lesson is the foundation of everything that follows.

The boardroom scene below is how this book begins—because the review is already happening, whether you show up for it or not.

The Interview You Didn't Know You Were In

"Thanks for coming in."

The room is clean. Quiet. Neutral. The kind of room where people don't waste words.

A folder is placed on the table in front of you. No logo. No small talk. No warm-up.

The interviewer looks at you the way a board looks at a leader when results are trending the wrong direction.

"Before we start," they say, "I want to clarify something. This isn't a motivational conversation. This is an operating conversation."

They open the folder.

"Tell me about your current performance."

You start where most people start—intentions.

"I'm trying to eat better. I'm working out when I can. I've been busy, but I'm getting back on track."

The interviewer doesn't react.

They slide a single page across the table.

"Show me the data."

You pause.

Because you don't have it. No baseline. No trendline. No early warning indicators. No risk register. Just a general feeling that you're mostly fine.

You're managing an enterprise with no visibility.

"Walk me through your recovery strategy," they say.

You answer quickly, like someone who's competent.

"I'll sleep more when things calm down. I'll get serious after this season."

They nod—not in agreement. In acknowledgment. Like they've heard this from every executive right before the breakdown.

Then they ask the question that changes the tone of the entire room:

"Do you believe you are currently qualified for this role?"

You start to respond—

And the interviewer closes the folder.

"Let me stop you there."

They lean forward.

"You're not applying for this job."

You blink.

"You already have it."

Hope is not a system.

There is no succession plan. There is no handoff. You cannot delegate this role.

"You report to reality," they say. "Not your calendar. Not your intentions. Not your motivation. Reality."

They slide the folder back toward you.

"Here's the good news. This isn't about shame. This is about clarity."

They tap the paper.

"Gaps are data. Skills are trainable. Systems solve it."

They stand.

"Read the job description. Then we build your CEO of Me Health Resume."

The folder opens. You see the title for the first time.

JOB DESCRIPTION

Chief Executive Officer—You, Inc.

Health, Performance, and Longevity Division

Location: Wherever your body is

Reports To: Reality

Direct Reports: Your habits, systems, and decisions

Term: Lifetime appointment

Retirement Plan: None

Role Summary

You are the Chief Executive Officer of the most valuable enterprise you will ever manage: your body.

This role carries full responsibility for the long-term performance, resilience, and sustainability of your physical, cognitive, and emotional operating systems. There is no succession plan. There is no handoff. Failure is slow, expensive, and rarely reversible.

You cannot delegate this role. You already hold it.

The only variable is whether you are operating intentionally or managing decline by default.

What This Role Requires

- Audit your health honestly—assess your baseline, identify risks, and govern from data, not feelings
- Execute consistently—build systems that function under pressure, travel, and disruption without relying on motivation
- Lead long-term—grow the enterprise's value over time. Every unmanaged liability compounds. Decline is not neutral.

- Leverage technology—use data tools, wearables, and AI to interpret health signals, design personalized protocols, and upgrade the system over time
- Recovery governance—demonstrated ability to treat sleep, stress management, and downtime as performance inputs, not optional rewards
- Health Resume maintenance—documented history of tracking competencies, measuring progress, and auditing performance on a defined cadence
- Adaptive execution—proven ability to modify the operating plan when conditions change without using disruption as justification to exit

Disqualifiers

- Treating health as a seasonal initiative
- Confusing effort with a system
- Waiting for a crisis to justify action
- Outsourcing accountability to a program or challenge without installing the underlying system
- Using "I'm busy" as a health strategy
- Treating this role as temporary

Performance Review

- Daily—execution check: commitments kept, standards protected, system running
- Weekly—reflection and adjustment: what drifted, what held, one correction made
- Quarterly—full health portfolio re-audit: what has improved, what has degraded, which risks have gone unaddressed
- Annual—strategic reset: goals reassessed, Health Resume updated, board composition evaluated

The Return

- Energy. Clarity. Physical independence. Longevity with capability.
- Full operational capacity—the ability to show up at complete

energy for work, family, and the life you are building

- Compounding health capital—assets that purchase options: what you can do, where you can go, how long you can lead
- A healthspan matched to lifespan—not just more years, but more years of genuine capability

Failure to perform results in:

- Declining cognitive output—reduced decision quality at the exact moments careers and relationships demand the most
- Compounding liability—the Pain Tax accelerates. What is manageable today becomes expensive and irreversible later
- System dependency—outsourcing to the medical system what governance and prevention could have addressed earlier
- Unrecoverable time loss—the one resource the role cannot recoup regardless of future performance
- A ceiling on every other enterprise—career, family, community— that depends on this one running

Final Note

This role does not end at retirement.

It ends when you do.

The question is not whether you are qualified today.

The question is whether you are willing to become qualified over time.

You sit across the table knowing this meeting is not about effort.

No one is asking how hard the year felt.
No one is asking how busy you were.
No one is asking how committed your intentions were.
The numbers are already on the screen.

What's being reviewed is output, resilience, risk, and trajectory. What worked. What was ignored too long. What assumptions quietly failed under pressure.

This is not a hostile meeting. It's worse than that. It's neutral.

Leadership is not measured by how difficult the role felt. It's measured by whether the system performed, whether risks were surfaced early, and whether it held when demand increased.

One question lands harder than the rest:

Which risks were accepted intentionally—and which were ignored by default?

There is no speech. No defense. No appeal to circumstances.

Just ownership.

Then it becomes clear.

This is not a boardroom review.
This is a health review.
The performance being evaluated is yours.

Your energy.
Your resilience.
Your recovery.
Your risk exposure.
Your trajectory over the long term.
Most people never experience this kind of review until the system breaks. By the time attention is forced, options are narrower and the cost is higher.

That delayed cost has a name: *the Pain Tax.*

You either pay now—in discipline, structure, and uncomfortable honesty—

or you pay later in fatigue, dependency, preventable diagnoses, and reduced options.

Either way, the bill comes due.

The difference isn't intelligence. It isn't effort.

It's governance.

I watched the Pain Tax collect in full from someone I loved—and that cost is what built this book.

No serious executive runs an organization without dashboards, audits, advisors, and a long-term strategy. Yet this is exactly how most people manage the most valuable asset they will ever own: their body.

This book exists to correct that.

That experience is why this book starts in a boardroom rather than a gym. Because the decision that cost my father his life was not a fitness decision. It was a leadership decision. And it made me ask: what would happen if someone applied the same rigor they bring to their business to the body running it? The next page shows you where that question leads.

The job description you just read is not aspirational. It is accurate. And like any serious role, it requires **competency**—not just intention.

Over the next ten chapters, you will build an **Executive Health Resume**: real capabilities that compound over time. How to assess. How to decide. How to execute. How to review and adapt.

Effort is not the credential.

Skill is.

The CEO of Me is not a fitness book, a diet book, or a motivation book.

It is an operating system.

The framework used throughout is the **Executive Health Operating System—EHOS**. It applies the same assessment, execution, review, and adaptation cycle used by high-performing organizations to the one enterprise that has no succession plan: your health.

No shortcuts.

No hacks.

No miracle products.

Just systems.

Systems outperform motivation every single time.

Your health is not a side project. It is the enterprise everything else depends on. There is no handoff. No retirement from this role.

You already hold the position.

The only question now is whether you run it—or let it run you.

You have the data. The next question is harder: what do you do with it before motivation disappears?

HOW TO USE THIS BOOK

This is not a book you read and set down.

It is a book you work through. There is a difference.

Each chapter follows the same architecture: a business story that frames the concept, a personal or client story that grounds it in real life, a named framework you can apply immediately, and an Operating Sheet at the end where you do the actual work. The Operating Sheet is not optional. It is where the chapter becomes yours.

The EHOS Dashboard

This book has a digital companion built specifically for it.

At adrianmwilliams.com, members can create a free account and access the EHOS Dashboard — currently in its launch phase — which mirrors every chapter in this book. As you complete each chapter, you log your Operating Sheet answers directly into the dashboard. Your responses are saved, organized by chapter, and compiled automatically into a dynamic CEO of Me Health Resume — a printable document that reflects your actual answers, your real standards, and the system you built.

The dashboard also includes:

A printable Operating Sheets pack — all 14 blank worksheets formatted for print, and four static reference resources: the EHOS Framework Overview, Weekly Review Checklist, SIS Reference Guide, and CEO Health KPI Tracker.

Create your free account before you begin Chapter 1. The dashboard is designed to be built alongside the book — not after you finish it.

The sequence that works best

Read the chapter first. Complete the Operating Sheet second.

Do not stop mid-chapter to fill in forms. Read all the way through, let the framework settle, then go to the Operating Sheet — in the book or in the dashboard — and complete it before moving to the next chapter. The system builds on itself. What you write in Chapter 1 informs Chapter 2. What you build in Chapter 2 informs everything that follows.

You do not have to start at Chapter 1.

If you are in the middle of a health breakdown, go to Chapter 6. If you have the habits but not the consistency, start at Chapter 9. If you have never had a real health strategy, Chapter 2 is your entry point. The EHOS framework is designed so each phase stands alone — but it is most powerful when you run all ten.

The Operating Sheets are your governance documents.

Treat them like that. Write in them. Be honest in them. A half-completed Operating Sheet is the same as a half-executed strategy — it looks like progress without producing any.

The Health Resume is the output.

At the back of this book is your CEO of Me Health Resume — a compiled record of every competency you build across ten chapters. In the dashboard, that resume compiles dynamically from your actual answers. By the time you reach it, it should not be blank. Every chapter you complete adds to it. That resume is the credential this book produces and the proof — to yourself — that you did the work.

One Final Note

This book will ask you to be honest in ways most health content does not. Honest about your data. Honest about your gaps. Honest about the distance between the standards you claim and the behavior you actually execute. That honesty is not a judgment. It is the starting point for everything that follows.

You already hold this role. This book teaches you how to run it.

— Adrian M. Williams

CHAPTER ONE

Assessing Your Health Portfolio

The audit comes first. Before strategy. Before execution. Before anything else.

Every effective turnaround starts the same way.

Before a CEO changes strategy, cuts costs, or launches a new initiative, there is a pause. Not a motivational pause. An honest one. The kind where assumptions are set aside and reality is examined without emotion.

What's actually working.

What's quietly breaking down.

What risks have been ignored because nothing has failed yet.

That pause is uncomfortable. And it's necessary.

Health deserves the same discipline. Most people never take it.

They go straight to action. A new workout. A new diet. A challenge they swear will finally be different this time. Effort increases, but clarity doesn't. They stay busy but unmanaged.

That's not leadership. That's reaction.

BlackBerry and the Cost of Ignoring Signals

In January 2007, the most powerful device in business was a BlackBerry. Not a phone. Not a computer. A BlackBerry. If you carried one, you were serious. Executives, government officials, heads of state—all of them locked in, thumbs moving.

Then Jobs held up the iPhone.

No keyboard. All glass. A touchscreen that responded like nothing anyone had seen.

BlackBerry's leadership watched the announcement. They were not worried. They were dismissive. Their engineers called it impractical. Executives pointed to their security infrastructure, their corporate contracts, their loyal user base. "Our customers need real keyboards," they said. "Touchscreens are a gimmick."

They were not lying. They believed it.

That belief—that what had always worked would keep working—is the most expensive assumption a leader can make.

BlackBerry's signals were everywhere. Developers were already gravitating toward Apple's platform. Consumer demand was shifting in real time. Early iPhone sales were telling a story the data made impossible to ignore—if you were looking.

BlackBerry was not looking.

Not because the information was hidden. Because confidence in past performance is the most comfortable blindfold there is. Their system had worked for years. Their customers were loyal. Nothing had failed yet.

Within a few years, their market share had collapsed. Not long after, they stopped making phones entirely. A category leader became a case study in what happens when leadership trusts its history more than its signals.

Here is what no one talks about in that story.

BlackBerry's problem was not the iPhone. The iPhone was just the consequence.

BlackBerry's problem was the decision made years earlier— the quiet, comfortable choice to stop auditing reality and start defending the past.

That decision did not feel like failure. It felt like confidence.

Your body can make the same choice—not dramatically, not with a press conference, but quietly, comfortably, with the same logic that ended BlackBerry: 'Things are mostly fine. I'll deal with it later.'

Past performance is not a health strategy. It is a delay tactic.

And like BlackBerry, by the time you feel the consequence, the window for easy correction has usually already closed.

This chapter exists to change that.

Before you build a turnaround plan—before strategy, before execution, before any of it—you audit the enterprise.

Kevin and the "Show Me the Data" Moment

Let me introduce you to Kevin.

Kevin is a creative designer in his twenties who works as a freelancer. His schedule was irregular, his stress was unpredictable, and his health habits were inconsistent. He came to me with the standard list of goals—lose weight, get leaner, increase his energy.

Kevin told me everything I needed to hear. He said he had cleaned up his eating. Started working out again. Was truly committed this time.

A few weeks into the program, he hit me with a line I have heard more times than I can count.

"I don't think this plan is working."

And a bit like Cuba Gooding, Jr., in that legendary scene from Jerry Maguire—"Show me the money"—I shot back with the only response that mattered: "Show me the data."

Kevin blinked. Laughed awkwardly. Then said something like, "I've been eating better and moving more."

I followed up. "Show me what you ate this week. Show me your workouts. Your sleep. Your stress levels. How much water you drank. Your recovery. Your heart rate. Anything measurable."

He had nothing.

"I can't fix what I don't know is broken," I told him. "You're guessing your way through this, and guessing is not a strategy. Right now, you are flying blind."

Kevin was not lazy. He was not unmotivated. He was trying to run a results-driven operation with no data, no system, and no visibility.

So we simplified everything. Each day, Kevin sent me a short text—photos of his meals, whether he trained or did not, hours of sleep, energy level, hydration, mood. Nothing complicated. Just the truth.

Four weeks later, the results showed up.

Same plan. Same effort. Different outcome.

That is the power of visibility. Even the best plan fails without it.

Data does not exist to shame you. It exists to protect you. A declining metric is not a failure. It is an early warning. Leaders do not ignore dashboard lights just because the car is still moving. They act before the engine fails.

The Story Behind This Book

The story that drove this book is in the opening pages—my father, the lump he recognized as cancer, the months he refused to see a doctor, the treatment that worked, and the relapse that didn't. You already know how it ends.

That experience taught me something I won't soften for you: most people don't fail because they don't care. They fail because they delay leadership. And delay always has a price.

> *That cost has a name I will come back to in Chapter 4—the Pain Tax. For now, understand this: every decision to wait is a decision to pay more later.*

This chapter exists because of that lesson.

Before you build a turnaround plan, you audit the enterprise.

Six in 10 adults in the United States live with at least one chronic disease. And 90 percent of the nation's $4.9 trillion in annual health care expenditures go toward people with chronic and mental health conditions—most of which are driven by preventable risk factors.[1] That is not a healthcare crisis. That is a leadership crisis. And it starts with the decision not to look.

Establishing the Baseline—Visibility Before Strategy

No executive builds a strategy without first establishing a baseline.

Before decisions are made, leaders ask one question: What do we actually know? Not what we feel. Not what we hope. Not what we assume. What we can verify.

Health deserves the same standard.

Most people think they know where they stand because they are trying. They are eating "better." Moving "more." Making an effort. But effort without visibility creates a dangerous illusion of control. You can be busy and still be exposed. You can be disciplined and still be misaligned.

In business, that is how companies fail quietly. In health, it is normalized.

Feelings Are Lagging Indicators

By the time you feel something is off, it has usually been off for a while.

Energy dips.
Sleep becomes lighter.
Stress lingers longer.
Recovery slows.
These are not sudden problems. They are delayed signals. Feelings are lagging indicators, and executives do not run organizations on lagging indicators alone.

If you are waiting until you feel bad to take action, you are already late.

Baselines change that. They turn guesswork into governance.

The Executive Health Operating System (EHOS)

This book runs on one system: the Executive Health Operating System—EHOS.

EHOS is not about perfection. It is about visibility, review, and adjustment over time—the same rhythm a high-performing CEO uses to run a company. Assess reality. Review performance. Make informed changes. Repeat consistently. Each chapter in this book activates a different phase of this loop—so by Chapter 10, the entire system is running.

One non-negotiable rule: you do not feel your way into strategy. You audit first.

Figure 1.1 *The EHOS Loop — Four Phases of the Executive Health Operating System*

Phase	Ask This	Non-Negotiable Rule
ASSESS Audit the Enterprise	What is the current state of my Health Portfolio? What risks am I ignoring because nothing has failed yet? What does my baseline actually show — without emotion?	You do not feel your way into strategy. You audit first.
REVIEW Interpret the Signals	What trends are improving, stable, or degrading? What patterns appear under stress, travel, or deadlines? What are my leading vs lagging indicators?	Feelings are lagging indicators. Data surfaces problems before they become expensive.
ADJUST Make CEO-Level Decisions	What is the single highest-leverage change this cycle? What will I stop doing to protect consistency? What is my contingency plan when pressure spikes?	One change at a time. Compound wins beat scattered effort.
REPEAT Cadence Beats Motivation	Daily: visibility check Weekly: Executive Review Monthly: deeper metrics Quarterly: portfolio re-audit	A system reviewed consistently outperforms a perfect plan reviewed never.

Pain Tax Trigger Question—ask it every week: "What am I delaying right now that will cost more later if I keep postponing it?"

Understanding Your Health Portfolio

A health portfolio is not a wellness vision board. It is a strategic, unsparing snapshot of your current health assets, liabilities, risks, and opportunities—reviewed the way a CEO reviews a business portfolio.

Your health portfolio includes six asset classes:

Figure 1.2 *Your Health Portfolio — Six Asset Classes*

Asset Class	What It Covers
Vital Metrics (KPIs)	Blood pressure, resting heart rate, weight, cholesterol, sleep quality
Lifestyle Investments	Nutrition, exercise, hydration, mobility, stress management
Health Liabilities	Poor sleep, chronic stress, sedentary patterns, untreated conditions
Return on Investment (ROI)	Energy, focus, resilience, mood, longevity
Risk Exposure	Genetic predispositions, environmental stressors, behavioral patterns under pressure
Strategic Support	Medical team, coaching, wearables, recovery tools, accountable relationships

A health portfolio is a living document. It evolves with your life. That is exactly why it requires active leadership—not periodic attention.

Think of it as your personal P&L statement.

Figure 1.3 *Health P&L — Assets vs. Liabilities*

P&L Category	Health Equivalent
Assets	Strong habits, clean biomarkers, healthy organ function
Liabilities	Genetic predispositions, chronic conditions, poor metrics
Net Revenue	Energy, focus, vitality, performance output
Expenses	Processed food, chronic stress, sleep debt, preventable illness

Your goal is the same as any CEO's: maximize revenue, minimize unnecessary expenses, and flag liabilities before they become failures.

Collect Your Data—The Annual Physical as Your Baseline Audit

Data collection starts with your annual physical.

We schedule ours around our birthdays—a simple recurring trigger that ensures we never skip it. But we do not stop at the medical appointment. Fitness applications and wearables track our daily patterns, workouts, and recovery in between.

Think of biomarkers from your annual physical as your health's KPIs. They tell you when something is a risk before it becomes a problem. They track everything from cardiovascular health to hormone balance to metabolic function.

Key biomarker categories to review with your physician:

Figure 1.4 *Biomarker Categories — Key Tests by Domain*

Category	Key Tests
Metabolic Health	Glucose, Insulin, HbA1c (long-term blood sugar control)
Cardiovascular	Total Cholesterol, HDL, LDL, Triglycerides, ApoB
Inflammation	CRP, Homocysteine, Ferritin
Hormonal	TSH, T3, T4 (thyroid), Testosterone, Cortisol
Nutrient Levels	Vitamin D, B12, Iron, Magnesium
Organ Function	ALT, AST (liver); Creatinine, eGFR (kidneys)
Other Screenings	Blood pressure, bone density, cancer screenings as appropriate

Note: The biomarkers listed above represent key indicators commonly used in executive health assessments—they are not exhaustive. Every body is different. Your physician will determine which panels are appropriate for your specific age, sex, medical history, and risk profile. Do not interpret these numbers in isolation. Bring this list to your next appointment and let your doctor translate the data into direction.

Your annual physical is the foundation. Wearables and fitness applications extend this visibility into your daily life. Chapter 7 covers the technology layer in detail. For now, collect what you can. Minimal data reviewed consistently beats perfect data reviewed never.

Analyze Like a Leader—The Personal Health SWOT

Once you have data, you analyze it the way a leader analyzes a business situation: systematically, without emotion, and with a bias toward action.

The tool for this is the Personal Health SWOT—adapted from executive strategy frameworks used to assess internal capabilities and external conditions.

Figure 1.5 *SWOT Dimensions — The Four-Quadrant Health Audit*

Dimension	The Question It Answers
Strengths (internal)	What health habits are working consistently right now?
Weaknesses (internal)	Where is performance degrading or risk accumulating?
Opportunities (external)	What leverage points exist to improve without overhauling everything?
Threats (external)	What pressures, habits, or patterns are eroding your baseline?

Audio book listeners and website visitors: download this table at adriannwilliams.com

Done correctly, a health SWOT removes emotion from the equation and replaces it with a map.

William's Turning Point

Business leaders use SWOT analysis as a guiding tool to make key decisions. As CEO of a consulting firm and the proud father of three boys, William has more than just business success on his mind—he's driven by the desire to be fully present and healthy for his family.

For him, leadership meant being present every day—with discipline, intention, and love—at home and at work.

When I began working with William, I asked about his intentions. He said he wanted more than accountability; he needed clarity. To help him align his actions with his deeper goals, we began with a personal SWOT analysis.

What emerged wasn't just a list of strengths and weaknesses, but a clearer vision of the man he's becoming—as a leader, and as a father.

William's Health SWOT—A Real Example

Figure 1.6 *William's Health SWOT — Real Example*

STRENGTHS	• Strong leadership and decision-making skills support disciplined health management. • Regular massages promote recovery and stress relief. • Strong emotional support system — family time, humor, and social engagement.
WEAKNESSES	• Time management strain due to balancing CEO duties and personal/family health. • Inconsistent dietary habits; difficulty resisting fast food under time pressure. • Work-life imbalance may compromise self-care, rest, and consistent exercise.
OPPORTUNITIES	• Strategic delegation at work to create more bandwidth for personal health priorities. • Use of digital health tools (apps, wearables, calendars) to reinforce accountability and routine. • Join wellness-focused CEO networks or masterminds to align health with executive peer culture.
THREATS	• High-performance stress associated with running a company may lead to chronic health consequences. • Family demands may conflict with professional and personal wellness schedules. • Burnout and overexertion due to a lack of boundaries and insufficient recovery time.

Nothing about this process was dramatic. That was the point.

The SWOT did not show William a failure. It showed him a gap—between the discipline he brought to every executive meeting and the

11

discipline he had quietly exempted his body from. Once he saw it that way, the path was obvious. Not comfortable. Obvious.

William did not leave with guilt. He left with a strategy.

Just like William, you are going to perform your own SWOT analysis.

What the Data Reveals—A Second Example

Jonathan was a fire instructor at the University of Maryland Fire and Rescue Institute—a role that required elite physical fitness and annual health evaluations. Pass the evaluation, keep your career. Miss a single metric, and you are sidelined with no set return date.

Jonathan's wake-up call came during one of those assessments. He looked fit by every external measure. But when the data came back, it told a different story. Resting heart rate elevated. Glucose spiked. LDL cholesterol above the threshold. Aerobic performance below passing. He did not feel sick. The data said otherwise. He was suspended from his role pending improvement.

That is when he was referred to me. Our first step was a full health portfolio audit—a complete diagnostic of his physiological KPIs. We integrated wearables to gather real-time data. What we found changed the approach entirely. His deep sleep scores collapsed on nights he consumed alcohol—even a single glass. His body composition revealed risk factors that a standard BMI reading had masked entirely. He was not just out of shape. His internal numbers told a different story than the mirror. No workout alone would solve that.

We removed alcohol for two weeks. His deep sleep rebounded. We layered in Zone 2 cardio—low-intensity, steady-state work that rebuilt his aerobic foundation without breaking down his recovery. We restructured nutrition around function, not appearance. Within three months, his key markers moved meaningfully in the right direction and he cleared the fitness threshold he needed. Jonathan did not just return to work. He came back better—and became the example for the recruits he trained.

The lesson Jonathan carried out wasn't about the numbers. It was about the gap between appearance and reality. He looked like a man in control. The data showed a system quietly failing. Assessment is what closed that gap—before his career, and his health, paid the price.

Your SWOT is in Operating Sheet 1. Complete it before moving to Chapter 2. The audit is the foundation—everything else builds on it.

This is where EHOS begins. The Executive Health Operating System starts with one non-negotiable: you cannot lead what you have not assessed. Everything you built in this chapter—your baseline, your SWOT, your first CEO decision—is the Assess step of the loop.

Assess. Review. Adjust. Repeat.

You just completed step one. Most people never do.

THREE ACTION STEPS

1. Schedule your annual physical this week. Not next month. This week. Put it on the calendar before you turn this page. It is the data your entire audit depends on.
2. Complete Operating Sheet 1 before starting Chapter 2. The SWOT only works if you finish it. A half-completed audit is the same as no audit. Give it 20 minutes. Be honest. That sheet is your starting baseline—everything in this book builds from it.
3. Write down your Pain Tax. One sentence. What have you been delaying that is already costing you? Name it. The cost does not disappear because you have not looked at it. Looking at it is how you stop paying interest.

Executive Debrief

OPERATING SHEET 1—YOUR HEALTH PORTFOLIO AUDIT

Complete this Operating Sheet in the book, or log your answers directly into the EHOS Dashboard at adrianmwilliams.com. Members with a free account can access all worksheets, save their responses by chapter, and generate their CEO of Me Health Resume automatically from their answers.

Executive Action 1—Schedule Your Annual Physical: If it is not on the calendar, it does not exist.

Executive Action 2—Your Personal Health SWOT: One entry per box minimum. No softening. Just the truth.

Figure 2.1 *EHOS Review Cadence — Daily, Weekly, Quarterly, Annual*

Cadence	KPI	Format	Rule
Daily (choose 3–5)	Sleep duration Sleep quality Energy level Steps / movement Hydration	Hours 1–5 score 1–5 score Count / mins On track / Off	If you track more than this, you will stop tracking. Minimal beats perfect.
Weekly (choose 1–2)	Training sessions Nutrition compliance	Count SIS days or planned vs unplanned	
Monthly / Quarterly (choose 1–3)	Resting heart rate Blood pressure trend Labs / biomarkers	Trend: ↑↓→ Trend: ↑↓→ With physician	Review with your medical advisor. Not every metric needs weekly eyes.

Figure 2.2 *Weekly Executive Review — 10 Questions in 10 Minutes*

1	What improved this week? Why?
2	What degraded this week? Why?
3	What did my data reveal that my emotions didn't?
4	What was my biggest risk exposure this week?
5	What pattern shows up under stress — sleep, food, training, screens?
6	What is one system change that would prevent that pattern next week?
7	What is the smallest next action that creates leverage?
8	What will I stop doing next week to protect consistency?
9	What is my one contingency plan if next week gets chaotic?
10	What am I delaying that will increase the Pain Tax if I keep postponing it?

Audio book listeners and website visitors: download this table at adrianmwilliams.com

Executive Action 3—Your First CEO Decision: Based on your SWOT, one liability you will address first. Not a list. One decision. This becomes your Chapter 2 turnaround strategy.

Congratulations—You've Earned These Skills

Health Portfolio Analyst—Conducted a full baseline audit across six health domains using objective data and a personal SWOT framework, replacing emotional self-assessment with evidence-based executive decision-making.

Health Risk Identifier—Diagnosed personal health liabilities and early-warning signals before they became operational failures, converting reactive crisis management into proactive risk governance.

Minimum Viable Execution Designer—Defined and deployed floor-level health standards for worst-week performance, ensuring the operating system never fully stops running regardless of conditions.

The strategy is next. Chapter 2 converts what you found in this audit into a plan that has a realistic chance of surviving contact with your actual life.

From Insight to Impact —
Your Strategic Health Turnaround Plan

The audit is done. Now you decide.

The audit is done. You have a baseline. You know where the gaps are. Now comes the move most people never make—they audit, feel motivated for a few days, then return to the same defaults.

Chapter 2 is where that pattern ends.

But an assessment without action is just a report.

Real change happens when insight turns into execution. And that starts with a single move: a decision. Not a resolution. Not a plan. A decision—the kind that does not require motivation to hold because it has been structured to survive without it.

Every turnaround—corporate or personal—begins at the same place. Not with luck. Not with a pep talk. With a choice. A deliberate, non-negotiable choice to lead differently.

Arianna Huffington and the Turnaround She Had to Lead Alone

In April 2007, Arianna Huffington was two years into building The Huffington Post into one of the fastest-growing media companies in the world. She was working 18-hour days, raising two teenage daughters, and running on the fuel that most high performers mistake for strategy: sheer force of will.

One morning, she stood up from her desk to get a sweater. She collapsed. When she came to, she was on the floor in a pool of blood, a broken cheekbone, stitches above her eye.

Weeks of medical tests followed. Specialists. Scans. The answer, when it finally came, was not a tumor or a cardiac event. It was a single word: burnout.

She had built an enterprise worth billions. She had run the most important enterprise she owned—herself—into the ground.

No investor could fix it. No consultant could step in. This was a turnaround only she could lead.

So she led it the way a CEO leads any serious turnaround: with clarity, structure, and a willingness to change what was not working regardless of how long it had been working before.

She realigned her mission—placing sustainable health at the center, not the margin, of her operating priorities. She started tracking sleep, recovery, and stress the way she tracked revenue. She built a personal advisory structure of experts and accountability. She reallocated her schedule and enforced recovery as a non-negotiable input to performance.

The result was not just recovery. It was a complete rebuild—one that eventually gave rise to Thrive Global, her company dedicated to ending the stress and burnout epidemic she had lived firsthand.

Transformation doesn't happen by accident. It begins with a decision. It is sustained by strategy. Before the strategy can hold, one question must be answered—and Chapter 3 opens with it.

Huffington did not wait for a second collapse. She made the decision while she still had options. That is the only difference between a turnaround and a tragedy.

That is the standard Chapter 2 is built on. Not the turnaround Huffington needed. The one you are choosing before you need it.

The Resume You've Never Written

Most people believe their health struggles are a motivation problem. They think they need more discipline. More willpower. More effort.

That assumption is almost always wrong.

In business, when a team keeps missing targets, a good leader does not immediately accuse them of not caring. They ask better questions. Are the systems clear? Are the skills developed? Are the expectations realistic given the conditions?

Health works the same way.

If your sleep is inconsistent, that is not a character flaw. It is a systems issue.

If your nutrition falls apart under stress, that is not laziness. It is a planning gap.

If your workouts disappear when life gets busy, that is not failure. It is a design problem.

Trying harder is a temporary solution. Skills create sustainability.

But effort is not a system. And effort is not a skill. That is why so many health plans collapse the moment life applies pressure.

As the CEO of your health, your job is not to try harder. Your job is to be qualified for the role.

The Effort vs. Skill Gap Matrix

Most people live in the upper-left quadrant: high effort, low skill. They work hard without upgrading their systems, then wonder why consistency collapses every time life applies pressure. The CEO Zone—the target quadrant—is not about working harder. It is about making the right systems durable enough to run under pressure.

Figure 2.3 *Effort vs. Skill Matrix — Identifying Your Highest-Return Move*

EFFORT → LOW   HIGH | SKILL ↓ LOW (bottom) to HIGH (top)

HIGH EFFORT / LOW SKILL	**HIGH EFFORT / HIGH SKILL**
Busy and Stuck	*CEO Zone*
Working hard without the right systems. Consistency collapses under pressure. The most common quadrant for high-achievers who haven't yet built health as a competency.	Effort is sustainable because systems are in place. Performance is repeatable. Recovery is planned. This is the target quadrant.
LOW EFFORT / LOW SKILL	**LOW EFFORT / HIGH SKILL**
Drifting	*Underperforming*
No system, no momentum. Reactive. The starting point for most people before they decide to lead.	The skills exist but aren't being deployed. Often seen after a long plateau or a period of coast-mode.

Building Your CEO of Me Health Resume

Every CEO operates with an implicit resume. It may not be written down, but it exists. It reflects what they are capable of managing, where they are strong, and where they rely on support or need development. No board would hire a CEO without understanding those capabilities.

Your health is no different.

Your habits, decisions, and consistency under pressure reveal what you are currently qualified to handle.

If you are inconsistent with sleep, you are underqualified in recovery management.

If you are reactive with food, you are underqualified in nutrition execution.

If stress keeps derailing you, you are underqualified in regulation and resilience.

This is not shame. This is clarity.

> *The gap between where you are and where you want to be is not a character flaw. It is a starting point. Every skill in this book was built by someone who started exactly where you are.*

The goal of EHOS is not perfection. The goal is capacity—a health resume that holds under pressure, not just during easy weeks.

EHOS Shifts Gears—From Assess to Adjust

In Chapter 1, you ran the ASSESS phase of EHOS. You audited the enterprise: portfolio view, baseline data, risk exposure, and a personal SWOT.

This is where EHOS shifts gears.

You've assessed. You've reviewed. Now you decide how to adjust and execute.

Not perfectly.

Not dramatically.

Strategically.

Turnarounds are strategic, not emotional. In business, a turnaround does not start with intensity. It starts with clarity.

What must change now.

What can wait.

What creates leverage.

What introduces risk.

You are not trying to win a quarter. You are trying to remain operational for decades. That requires planning with the long game in mind.

The Turnaround Blueprint—Four Phases

This is your strategic health plan, structured the way a corporate turnaround is structured: four phases, each one building on the last, each one designed to survive pressure.

Figure 2.4 *The Turnaround Blueprint — Four-Phase Framework*

Phase	The CEO's Question	Your Health Version
1 — Vision & Mission	Where are we going and what do we commit to weekly?	What does "operational" look like in 12–36 months? What will you do consistently to get there? A vision without a mission is just a wish.
2 — Priority Initiatives	What 2–3 moves create the most leverage right now?	Sleep, nutrition, training, stress management, preventive care. Pick the ones bleeding most. In business, you don't fund everything. You fund what moves the needle.
3 — SMART Goals	What does success look like at 30, 90, and 365 days?	Specific. Measurable. Reality-tested. Designed for your real week, not a perfect one. Short-term builds momentum. Long-term builds direction.
4 — Risk Controls	What breaks execution under pressure — and what's the pre-built response?	If [disruption], then [minimum plan]. Else [standard plan]. Written before you need it. You don't leave execution to mood.

Phase 1: Vision and Mission

Your vision is where you are going. Your mission is what you commit to doing consistently to get there.

A vision without a mission is just a wish. Most health plans fail at this stage because they set a destination without defining the weekly operating behavior that makes it reachable.

Your mission is not "eat healthier." It is a specific weekly commitment: three strength sessions, SIS meals on weekdays, eight hours of sleep as a protected boundary. Concrete. Repeatable. Measurable.

Vision—one sentence. Where is this enterprise headed? Not a mood board. A stated destination you can measure your decisions against.

My vision: remain healthy, independent, and strong as I age.

Mission—the specific operating commitments that close the gap between where you are and where that vision requires you to be. Ask yourself what you are actually trying to achieve:

- Reduce known risk factors—blood pressure, glucose, weight?
- Build performance capacity—stamina, strength, cognitive output?
- Protect mobility and independence as you age?

Your mission is the answer to that question translated into weekly behavior.

Phase 2: Prioritize Health Initiatives

In business, you do not fund everything. You fund what moves the needle. The same discipline applies here.

Look at your audit from Chapter 1. What is bleeding most? What single improvement would create the largest cascade of other improvements? That is your lead initiative.

Pick two or three initiatives maximum. More than three is not a strategy. It is a wishlist.

Phase 3: SMART Goals Across Timelines

Short-term goals build momentum. Long-term goals build direction. Your goals must be specific, measurable, and designed for your real life—not a perfect week. SMART goals are Specific, Measurable, Achievable, Relevant, and Time-bound. Not 'sleep more'—but 'in bed by 10:30 PM on weeknights, 5 nights out of 7, for the next 30 days.' Specificity is what separates a wish from a target.

Great leaders do not just dream big. They structure goals across timelines. Quick wins to stabilize. Mid-range milestones to build momentum. Long-term targets that shape the future of the enterprise.

Your health deserves the same architecture.

Phase 4: Risk Controls—If / Then / Else

This is where execution becomes real.

Back in my programming days, I learned early that logic protects outcomes. If this happens, then I do this. Else, I do that. Clean. Pre-decided. No negotiation in the moment.

That same principle belongs in your health turnaround. You do not leave execution to mood.

If travel happens, then I execute the travel version of my plan. Else I run my standard plan.

If sleep gets disrupted, then I adjust training intensity. Else I keep progression.

If stress spikes, then I switch to regulation-first mode. Else I stay on offense.

You build conditional systems that hold under pressure. Pre-written, pre-decided, pre-committed. By the time disruption arrives, the decision has already been made.

James and the Strategic Sleep Pivot

James was a husband, a father of three, working a demanding full-time job while carrying a full MBA course load. He was in his late forties and had been averaging three to four hours of sleep a night for nearly two years.

He was doing what most high performers do when life gets crowded.

He cut sleep first.

He was not lazy. He was ambitious. He was grinding. He was trying to win on every front simultaneously—career, education, family. On paper, he was doing it all. In reality, he was running on fumes and could not understand why.

His energy was gone. His focus at work was slipping. He could not stay sharp in class or stay present with his family. He assumed the issue was time management.

The real problem was simpler. And far more expensive.

James had never built sleep into his strategy. He treated it as the budget line he could cut when pressure arrived. What he did not understand was that sleep was not a recovery expense. It was his highest-return investment.

Research consistently shows that sleep deprivation impairs decision-making quality, increases risk-taking, and degrades the executive functions of the prefrontal cortex—the exact capabilities James needed most.[1]

We did not start by adding more workouts or building a more complicated nutrition plan.

We started by restoring the foundation: sleep.

James reduced his MBA course load. He made sleep non-negotiable. He built a hard stop time and protected it.

Within weeks, the cascade began. Decision-making improved. Cravings lowered. Training became more consistent. Stress became more manageable. His energy stopped being unpredictable. He was more present with his wife and children.

One priority change. Everything else followed.

> *The CEO move wasn't intensity. It was leverage. Sleep was the highest-return initiative in his portfolio. In EHOS terms, James did what Chapter 2 asks every reader to do: he reviewed what the audit revealed, identified the highest-leverage adjustment, and built a system around it. That is the Adjust step. That is the turnaround.*

THREE ACTION STEPS

1. Complete your Turnaround Blueprint. One page. Four phases. Use the Operating Sheet at the end of this chapter. Vision, mission, two to three priority initiatives, SMART goals at 30, 90, and 365 days, and at least three If/Then/Else risk controls written before disruption arrives.
2. Write your CEO of Me Health Resume snapshot. Identify two current strengths and two to three skill gaps using the matrix from this chapter. Be honest. Gaps are data, not verdicts. Name the system you will install to close the most important gap this month.
3. Identify your highest-return initiative. Look at your audit from Chapter 1. What is the single priority change that would create the largest cascade of improvement in everything else? Sleep, stress, nutrition, movement—which one is your James moment? Start there.

EXECUTIVE DEBRIEF

A turnaround starts the moment you decide the enterprise matters enough to lead—before conditions are comfortable, before motivation arrives, before anyone gives you permission. Huffington did not wait for a second collapse. You did not either.

"The plan is not the turnaround. Execution is."

The Turnaround Blueprint

Purpose: Build your four-phase strategic health plan. Complete all four phases before moving to Chapter 3.

CEO Standard: A plan that lives only in your head is not a plan. It is a preference. Write it down.

Operating Sheet 2.2

The CEO of Me Health Resume

Purpose: Identify your current health competencies and your most important skill gap. Build the upskill plan that closes it.

Rule: Gaps are data. Skills are trainable. Systems solve it. Pick the highest-leverage gap and install one system this month.

Congratulations—You've Earned These Skills

Health Strategist—Designed a long-term personal health mission and turnaround plan aligned to life demands and leadership values, replacing reactive health management with a structured, milestone-sequenced strategic framework.

Health Performance Planner—Built a 30/60/90-day health execution roadmap with defined KPIs, review checkpoints, and success metrics, creating a governance structure that survives real-world schedule pressure.

Phase	Your Answer
Vision (12–36 months) Where are you going?	_______________________________ _______________________________
Mission (weekly commitments) What will you do consistently?	_______________________________ _______________________________
Priority Initiative #1 KPI:	Initiative: _______________________ KPI to track: _____________________
Priority Initiative #2 KPI:	Initiative: _______________________ KPI to track: _____________________
Priority Initiative #3 (optional) KPI:	Initiative: _______________________ KPI to track: _____________________
30-Day Goal	_______________________________
90-Day Goal	_______________________________
12-Month Goal	_______________________________
Risk Control #1 If ___, then ___, else ___	If: _____________________________ Then: ___________________________ Else: ___________________________
Risk Control #2 If ___, then ___, else ___	If: _____________________________ Then: ___________________________ Else: ___________________________
Risk Control #3 If ___, then ___, else ___	If: _____________________________ Then: ___________________________ Else: ___________________________

Health Accountability Designer—Established personal reporting structures, review cadences, and board-level oversight to sustain execution consistency across changing life conditions.

A PLAN ON PAPER IS STILL A PREFERENCE. CHAPTER 3 IS WHERE IT MEETS MONDAY MORNING.

Capability Area	Your Assessment
Current Strength #1	Skill: ____ Evidence (what I execute consistently): _______________
Current Strength #2	Skill: ____ Evidence: ____
Skill Gap #1	Gap: ____ What breaks down: _________________________________
Skill Gap #2	Gap: ____ What breaks down: _________________________________
Skill Gap #3 (optional)	Gap: ____ What breaks down: _________________________________
Upskill Plan — Next 30 Days	Skill to build: _____________________________________ System to install: __________________________________ KPI to track: ______________________________________ Review cadence: ___________________________________

CHAPTER THREE

Operational Wellness Overhaul

—

Build the System That Runs When You're Not Looking

Strategy tells you where to go. Operations get you there every day.

You have assessed. You have built the strategy. Now EHOS shifts into its third gear—execution.

This chapter is where the strategy meets the calendar.

Assessment without execution is just a report. Strategy without operations is just a plan. What separates leaders who get results from those who stay stuck in planning mode is one thing: the daily operating system.

But before we build it, there is one question that must be answered first.

Not "what will you do."

Why will you keep doing it when it gets hard.

The Foundation That Holds When Motivation Doesn't

Every operating system has a load-bearing wall. The structure collapses without it. In EHOS, that wall is your WHY—not a goal, not a mood board, not a mission statement you type and forget. The specific, non-negotiable reason this system has to keep running when the alarm goes off early, the meeting runs late, and the plan meets a week that had other ideas.

This is where most health efforts fail.

Diets, workout plans, and even advanced fitness technology can create short bursts of motivation. But motivation is fragile. Stress, setbacks, deadlines, family obligations, and uncertainty will test it. Only a deeply personal WHY—one that is emotional, mission-critical, and non-negotiable—holds when conditions are no longer ideal.

In business, no serious investor backs a company without a clear mission and a resilient foundation. Your health deserves the same rigor. Without a WHY, you are not leading your life—you are gambling with it. Strategy without a WHY becomes busyness. Health without a WHY becomes wishful thinking.

Before you take on another challenge, pause and ask yourself a harder question:

Because the future CEO of You, Inc. will only be as strong as the foundation you set now.

This is not about motivation. This is about durability.

Real-World WHYs: The Weight of a Reason

I was in the gym waiting for a client when a man on the power tower caught my attention.

He was moving through pull-ups, chin-ups, and dips with incredible control. He had on a tank top and was chiseled like a gymnast. For twenty or thirty minutes he stayed on that station, and when he needed a break he did not come down. He rested his forearms on the arm pads, then kept going.

His shirt caught my eye first.

On the front it said: "Be grateful for what you have." On the back: "Not what you don't have."

I walked over and asked if he had been a gymnast. He smiled and said no. Then I noticed the wheelchair behind him.

He told me he was former military, injured in Iraq, and had lost the use of his legs. Before the injury, he and his three closest friends—brothers to him—used to compete on exercises just like those, betting on who could do the most pull-ups, chin-ups, and dips.

They did not all make it home.

So now every set is for one of them. One for himself. Three for the brothers he lost.

"I may not have my legs, but I have my arms. I have my life. And I am grateful for that."

That was his WHY. He was not just working out. He was honoring the men who no longer could.

His system did not run on motivation. It ran on mission. A mission does not need a good day to execute. That is the standard your WHY has to meet—not inspirational enough to share, but durable enough to run on your worst week.

That is what a real WHY looks like inside EHOS—the load-bearing wall that holds the entire operating system up when everything else tries to pull it down.

My WHY

I do not train because I love every morning. I train because I have watched what happens when a man does not.

My WHY is simple. It is not about looking a certain way or hitting a number on a scale. It is about being there. Fully there. Not as a burden on the people who love me most—my wife, my children, my family— who would show up for me without hesitation and deserve better than watching me decline from choices I could have made differently.

I cannot prevent everything. I know that. Life does not come with guarantees. But there is a difference between what happens to you and what you allow to happen through neglect. I refuse to be the author of my own breakdown. Not when the pen is in my hand.

What drives me is simple: I want my healthspan to match my lifespan. Not just more years. More good years. Years where I am strong, present, and capable. Where I can move without pain, think without fog, and show up for the people I love without being the reason they worry. Where I get to be a husband, a father, a grandfather—not a patient.

Every intentional meal—built around whole, single-ingredient foods—is a vote for the version of me that shows up at full capacity. That is not discipline. That is love expressed as a system.

When the alarm goes off at 4:15 a.m. and nothing wants to move, that is what moves me. When travel makes it inconvenient and the excuses stack up, that is what clears them. A WHY you can negotiate away when life gets hard was never a WHY. It was a preference. Yours needs the same weight.

A Deeper WHY: When Commitment Becomes Non-Negotiable

Another experience drove this principle even deeper for me.

I was preparing to give a speech at NABA's regional conference in Chicago. I went to the hotel gym for my 5:00 a.m. workout. As I was finishing, I noticed an older woman—likely in her mid to late seventies—come in. She walked on the treadmill for a few minutes, did some stretching, lifted a few weights.

As we were both leaving, she asked if I had a good workout. I said yes and returned the question. She smiled and said it wasn't her best, but she did something, and she kept her promise.

I asked what promise she meant.

She told me she had promised God that if she survived cancer, she would never take her health for granted again.

That day, she committed to a completely different life. She became a vegetarian. She gave up drinking and smoking. She moved her body every day. Twenty years later, she was still cancer-free.

That wasn't motivation. That was commitment.

A life-defining WHY.
A reason larger than inconvenience.
A foundation strong enough to hold under pressure.
Your WHY must be personal. It must be emotional. And it must be non-negotiable.

Because when pressure rises—and it will—you won't rise to your goals. You'll fall back to your standards. If your WHY is shallow, your standards will collapse under stress.

The WHY is not a motivational poster. It is structural. It is the load-bearing wall of your operating system. Everything else—the cadence, the SIS meals, the minimum viable workouts, the contingencies—is only as durable as the reason underneath it.

Without a WHY, you're not leading your health. You're just trying harder until you stop.

From Grit to Systems—The Operational Overhaul

By the late 1970s, U.S. special operations forces were known for toughness, not efficiency. Training was brutal. Attrition was high. Success depended heavily on pain tolerance and endurance. The culture rewarded suffering more than preparation.

Then came a reckoning.

After the failed April 1980 Iran hostage rescue mission—Operation Eagle Claw—it became clear that grit alone was not enough. Eight servicemen were killed. The mission failed not because the operators lacked courage, but because the systems lacked coordination. The official investigation cited deficiencies in mission planning, command and control, and inter-service operability. (The Holloway Report, Joint Chiefs of Staff, 1980)

What followed was a complete operational overhaul.

Special operations forces stopped relying on punishment as preparation. They began operating like high-performing organizations. After-action reviews were embedded after every mission and training evolution. Data replaced gut instinct. Recovery, sleep, and nutrition were reclassified as strategic assets. Precision replaced brute force. The overhaul produced a new model for elite operations—one built on systems, rehearsal, and debrief rather than individual heroics.

Failure was no longer something to hide or endure. It became feedback.

They did not become elite by working harder. They became elite by building systems that held up under chaos.

Most people approach health the way those forces once approached training. They rely on grit. They push harder. They treat exhaustion as evidence of commitment. Then life applies pressure and the system collapses.

That is not a discipline problem.

That is an operational failure.

Your health deserves the same overhaul. Discipline is raw potential.

Without systems, it burns out. Without structure, it produces inconsistency. Without recovery, it creates breakdown instead of resilience.

You are no longer managing your health through willpower. You are rebuilding it as an operating system. That operating system has a name: EHOS. And like the special operations overhaul, it runs on standards, not suffering.

The Operational Rhythm

Successful CEOs manage their schedules because time is the real currency. If you have time for social media or television, you have time for movement. The question is not time. It is governance.

Your goal is simple: build a default operating rhythm that survives your real week. Not your perfect week. Your real week.

A cadence has three parts:

- Non-negotiables—the baseline you protect regardless of what else is happening
- Defaults—what you execute automatically when life gets chaotic
- Review rhythm—the weekly check that prevents drift before it becomes a trend. That review rhythm is EHOS in its daily form—the Assess and Review steps built into the week so drift gets caught before it compounds.

Here is how we approach it.

My alarm goes off at 4:15 a.m. By 5:00 a.m. I am leading a group workout that fosters accountability, community, and consistency. My wife and I then train together from 6:15 a.m. to 7:00 a.m. After training, we take 5 to 10 minutes to brief each other. We align schedules, plan meals, anticipate stressors, and decide how we will protect the standard when the day tries to take it.

You can do a version of this without copying our exact routine.

The point is not the time on the clock.

The point is the rhythm.

A rhythm does not require perfection. It requires repeatability. The CEO who runs their operations on a consistent review cadence outperforms the one who reacts to whatever arrives first. Your health cadence works the same way.

Anthony and the System Failure Week

Most people try to win at health with willpower.

That is like trying to run a company on motivation. It works until pressure hits.

If you want consistency, you build habit infrastructure. James Clear's research in Atomic Habits identifies four laws of lasting behavior change: make the right choice obvious, attractive, easy, and satisfying.[2] The CEO translation is simpler: your environment is your operating system. If your environment is built for drift, drift is what you get.

Anthony is a top executive. Smart. Driven. High-output.

He told me the same thing I hear from high performers all the time:

"Adrian, I know what to do. I just need to be more consistent."

That sentence is a trap. Because in health, "more consistent" almost always means "more dependent on perfect conditions."

Anthony's routine worked when life was calm. He trained early, ate clean, and stayed on track.

Then a real week hit.

Two late-night meetings. A flight delay. A deadline. A client escalation. He missed one workout, then two. He grabbed food between calls. Sleep dropped. Caffeine went up. His mood got shorter. His patience got thinner. He did not "fall off." His system reverted to default.

By Friday, he texted me:

"I don't know how this happened. I was doing great."

I told him the truth.

"It happened the same way every breach happens. Not because you didn't care. Because the procedure wasn't built to survive pressure."

So I made it undeniable. I asked for his week.

What did you eat Monday?
What time did you go to bed?
How many steps did you take?
What was the plan when meetings ran late?
There was no plan. There was hope.

| *Hope is not an operating system.*

That is when we rebuilt his operations around one principle:

Your plan is not real until it works on your worst week.

We installed a Minimum Viable Day. Three non-negotiables he could execute even when everything else was chaotic:

- Movement minimum: 12 minutes. No negotiation.
- SIS baseline meal: one default meal he could repeat without thinking.
- Recovery minimum: screens down at a fixed time and a hard bedtime window.

Then we added contingencies:

If meetings ran late, then he walked after the last call.
If travel hit, then he used the hotel gym for a minimum viable session.
If sleep was under six hours, then he kept training light and protected recovery.
Three weeks later, he did not magically become motivated.

He became operational.

His weight stabilized. His energy stopped swinging. He trained consistently without needing perfect mornings. His stress did not disappear, but it stopped hijacking the system.

That is the difference between discipline and design.

> *Discipline breaks when life gets loud. Systems don't.*

Build Your Minimum Viable Day

Your Minimum Viable Day is in Operating Sheet 3.1. Fill it in before this chapter ends—not after you need it.

Figure 3.1 *Minimum Viable Day — Three Non-Negotiables*

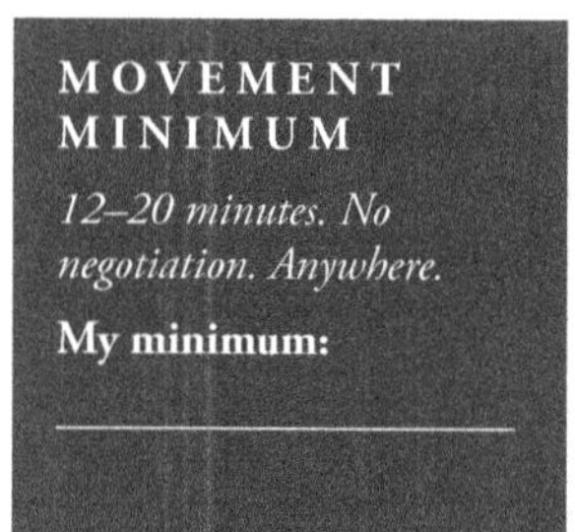

NUTRITION MINIMUM
One SIS meal or baseline meal. No winging it.
My minimum:

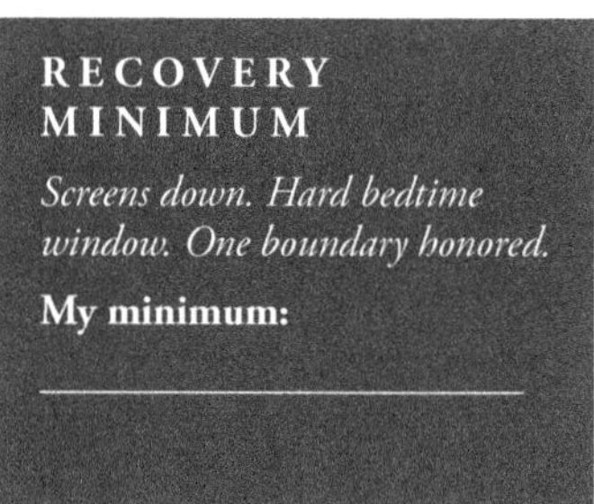

Audio book listeners and website visitors, download this table at adrianmwilliams.com

One test: if you cannot execute your Minimum Viable Day on your worst week, the plan is too complex. Simplify until you can run it half-asleep.

SECTION 5—SIS: THE SINGLE INGREDIENT STANDARD

SIS—The Single Ingredient Standard

I call this the Single Ingredient Standard—SIS. One rule. One filter. Binary by design.

SIS is not a diet.

It is procurement discipline.

The rule is clean:

> *If a food has more than one ingredient, it does not meet the Single Ingredient Standard.*

That is it. Simple. Binary. No judgment. Just clarity.

SIS works because it removes ambiguity. It reduces decision fatigue. It stabilizes your inputs so your outcomes stabilize. It turns eating into governance, not guessing. And because whole foods tend to be more filling and less calorie-dense than processed alternatives, following SIS as your baseline makes it harder to consistently overeat—without requiring you to count a single calorie.

This is how high-performing leaders win operationally. They standardize what matters so the decision is made once, not every meal.

Your food procurement becomes consistent enough to stop draining mental energy—which means more capacity for everything else.

Your goal is not perfection. Your goal is a baseline that runs on autopilot.

The Rule of One—Four Pillars

SIS is not just a grocery filter. It is a full decision-making framework that scales across meals, travel, restaurants, and high-pressure weeks.

Figure 3.2 *SIS — The Four Pillars of the Single Ingredient Standard*

Pillar	The Rule	Real-World Example
1 — One Ingredient	Choose foods in their original, unprocessed form. Single ingredient = single decision. Multiple ingredients = multiple risks.	Chicken. Eggs. Oats. Apples. Sweet potato. If you can't name every ingredient from memory, it's a risk.
2 — One Plate	Eat meals you can visually quantify. Full plate. No tiny portions. No starvation logic. Satisfaction is part of sustainability.	Grilled salmon + roasted vegetables + rice. You can see everything on the plate. Nothing hidden.
3 — One Choice Ahead	Always make the next best decision. SIS removes shame and focuses on momentum. You don't restart. You re-enter.	You ate off-plan at lunch. SIS dinner puts you back on standard. One meal never defines the week.
4 — One Percent Better	Small improvements compound over time. SIS wins long-term through consistency, not intensity. The standard is the strategy.	Replace one processed snack with a SIS option. Repeat for 30 days. The system builds without you forcing it.

SIS in the real world: At a restaurant, order the simplest preparation—grilled protein, roasted vegetable, rice or potato. Nothing hidden. On travel, eggs, fruit, chicken, and water are SIS-approved in any airport or hotel. Under stress, SIS does not demand perfection. It demands a standard. One SIS meal puts you back on track.

Minimum Viable Workouts

The best program is the one you execute consistently.

Not the one you save on Instagram. Not the one you promise to start when life slows down.

Training needs to fit your calendar, your joints, and your life stage. That is the operational approach.

You are building a weekly rhythm that can scale:
- Strength work—two to three sessions per week as the foundation
- Conditioning—one to two sessions, adjusted to life stage and recovery
- Mobility and recovery—non-negotiable, not optional

You also need a minimum viable workout for chaotic days. Because chaotic days are not exceptions. They are the environment.

A 12 to 20 minute bodyweight circuit counts. A brisk walk with a weighted vest counts. A hotel room floor workout counts. What does not count is skipping because the conditions were not perfect.

The Morocco Test

Tasha was in Morocco for business. I had time to explore.

The hotel was five stars. The gym was one star— and it looked nothing like the picture. The equipment looked like it had survived both World Wars. Whatever machines were still standing had no business being called functional. I stood there for a moment trying to figure out my options.

Then I stopped trying to recreate what I do at home and used what was there. Bodyweight work. Whatever equipment still functioned. And then I went outside.

The locals did not use gyms. They walked everywhere. They rode bikes. Movement was not a scheduled event for them—it was just how they lived. So I joined them. I walked neighborhoods I would never have seen from a resort pool. I rented a bike and rode until I did not know where I was. It was the best workout of the trip.

> *Your routine is only real if it works when nothing goes your way.*

When we were kids, nobody asked to go outside to work out. We just wanted to go outside. Walking, riding bikes, running around—that was just playing. And somehow we stayed in shape without a program, a plan, or a gym membership. Most countries where people walk and ride bikes everywhere do not call it exercise. It is just life. That is the version of movement that lasts—not the kind you schedule, but the kind that becomes who you are.

SECTION 7—RECOVERY IS A STRATEGY

Protect Recovery Like Revenue

Most people treat recovery as optional. Something they will do when there is time.

There is never time. You protect it or you lose it.

In business, scheduled maintenance is not a luxury. It is how you keep the machine running. Your health is no different. Recovery is when adaptation happens, when tissue repairs, when the nervous system resets, when the prefrontal cortex restores the decision-making capacity that pressure depletes.[3]

We do not "earn" our health habits. We install them. Our baseline includes daily movement, mobility, hydration, nutrition discipline, sleep protection, and a mental reset—stretching and mindfulness included. Recovery is scheduled, not improvised. Spa time, saunas, and rest days are standard operating procedure, not a bonus.

The CEO who consistently recovers well makes better decisions. Carries less reactive stress into the room. Leads with more clarity and less friction.

Recovery is not what you do after performance. Recovery is what makes performance possible.

Contingencies, Not Excuses

You built the risk controls in Chapter 2. This section is where they become automatic.

A real operating system includes contingencies. Because disruption is not a surprise. It is a guarantee.

Amateurs improvise their health under pressure. Professionals run a plan.

So you pre-write your responses:

If travel happens, then I do my minimum viable workout. Else I run my full training plan.

If late meetings happen, then I walk after the last call. Else I train at my scheduled time.

If stress spikes, then I switch to regulation-first mode. Else I stay on the standard plan.

If sleep is under six hours, then I keep training light and protect recovery. Else I keep progression.

This is what separates execution from intention. Not the plan itself—but the pre-written decision that runs when conditions are imperfect.

Write your contingencies before you need them. By the time disruption arrives, the decision has already been made.

1. Write your WHY. One sentence. Personal, emotional, non-negotiable. Post it somewhere you will see it on your hardest days. This is the load-bearing wall. Everything else sits on top of it.
2. Build your Minimum Viable Day. Three non-negotiables: movement minimum, nutrition minimum, recovery minimum. Use the card in this chapter. Fill it in before this week ends. This is what you run when life gets loud.
3. Write three If/Then/Else contingencies for the three disruptions that reliably derail you. Travel. Late meetings. High-stress days. One sentence each. Pre-decided. Non-negotiable.

EXECUTIVE DEBRIEF

Strategy without operations is just a plan. Chapter 3 gave you the operating layer—the daily cadence, the minimum viable standards, the SIS baseline, and the contingencies that run automatically when pressure arrives. The WHY holds it together. The system makes it run without you.

"Discipline breaks when life gets loud. Systems don't."

OPERATING SHEET 3.1

The Operational Rhythm—EHOS Execution Layer

Purpose: Build a default health cadence that survives your real week without relying on motivation.

CEO Standard: No review means no leadership. Review is how you prevent drift. Schedule it like revenue.

Operating Sheet 3.2

SIS + Training + Recovery—One-Page Control Panel

Purpose: Reduce decision fatigue by standardizing inputs and protecting recovery. Fill this in once. Run it every week.

Rule: If recovery breaks, output breaks next. Protect it like revenue.

Congratulations—You've Earned These Skills

Health Operations Manager—Built and executed a daily health operating cadence—including nutrition standards, movement minimums, and recovery protocols—that runs consistently regardless of motivation level or schedule disruption.

Element	Your Answer
Non-Negotiable #1 Daily movement	What I will do: ______________________ Minimum version: ______________________
Non-Negotiable #2 One healthy meal	What I will eat: ______________________ Backup option: ______________________
Non-Negotiable #3 Stress downshift or recovery	What I will do: ______________________ Time I will protect: ______________________
My Minimum Viable Day (when everything is chaotic)	Movement: ______________________ Nutrition: ______________________ Recovery: ______________________
Weekly Executive Review Same day, same time	Day: _________ Time: _____________ CEO Standard: no review = no leadership
Contingency #1 If ___, then ___. Else ___.	If: ______________________ Then: ______________________ Else: ______________________
Contingency #2 If ___, then ___. Else ___.	If: ______________________ Then: ______________________ Else: ______________________
Contingency #3 If ___, then ___. Else ___.	If: ______________________ Then: ______________________ Else: ______________________

Nutrition Governance Specialist—Implemented the Single Ingredient Standard as a binary nutrition decision framework, eliminating daily food decision fatigue and stabilizing dietary inputs without requiring willpower at the point of execution.

Minimum Viable Execution Designer—Defined and deployed floor-level health standards for worst-week performance, ensuring the operating system never fully stops running regardless of conditions.

Figure 3.4 *SIS Procurement Standards — Weekly Defaults*

Area	My Standard
SIS Procurement Rule (daily default)	My rule: ____ 80/20 standard: __________ % SIS, ________ % flex
My 3 Baseline Meals (repeatable, not fancy)	Breakfast: ____ Lunch: ____ Dinner: ____
Weekly Training Rhythm (realistic target)	Strength: ______ days Cardio/Conditioning: ______ days Mobility/Recovery: ______ days
Minimum Viable Workout (15–20 min, any location)	What I will do: ____________________________________ Example: circuit, walk + bodyweight, mobility flow
Recovery KPIs (pick 3–5)	Sleep window consistency: ______ nights/week Energy (1–5): ______ average Rest days: ______ /week Other: ____
Recovery Boundary (non-negotiable)	My boundary: _____________________________________ Rule: if recovery breaks, output breaks next.

Rule: If recovery breaks, output breaks next. Protect it like revenue.

CHAPTER FOUR

Health Investment and ROI —
Your Body Is the Asset. Treat It Like One.

In business, investments are judged by results. Health is no different.

The system is running. EHOS now shifts from execution into investment thinking—because operating the enterprise is not enough. You have to grow it.

Operations keep the machine running. Investment determines how well it runs—and for how long.

Most people treat health like an expense. Something to manage, minimize, or defer when other priorities compete for the budget. That frame is the problem. An expense is a cost. An investment is a return. When you stop thinking about your health as a cost and start managing it as capital, everything changes: the decisions you make, the things you fund, the things you cut, and the timeline you are willing to hold.

This chapter is where the shift happens.

ROI Is a Mindset First—Then Math

Most people never apply investment logic to their health because they do not see their body as an asset worth investing in. That is the mindset shift. Once you make it, the math becomes unavoidable.

Health works the same way. It is not about what you think you are investing. It is about what that investment yields.

I learned this firsthand.

After tearing and then rupturing my Achilles, I trained for the Cherry Blossom 10-Miler. I had to learn how to walk again, but my goal was to run again. So when I worked my way down to 12 minute miles, it felt like progress. It felt like I was back in business.

I told a coworker my pace.

He nodded like I had just described his warm up and casually offered to join me "on his slow day."

On his slow day.

I was insulted. Not quietly. Internally, I was offended on principle. I did not hear encouragement. I heard disrespect.

Here is what made it worse. He had been running consistently for over five years. His pace was a seven-minute mile. He had never been injured.

In that moment, I missed the obvious. His pace was not talent. It was compounded investment. Years of deposits: consistent training, disciplined recovery, and injury-free execution. My investment timeline had just restarted. I was rebuilding from a rupture.

But instead of respecting that timeline, I tried to mimic his returns without matching his deposits.

And I paid for it. I pulled my hamstring and it set me back for weeks.

That lesson was clear:

> *I have to run my race. No one else's. The mindset shift came first: I had to stop seeing his seven-minute mile as a comparison and start seeing my twelve-minute mile as a starting deposit.*

ROI is not a mindset. It is math. If you do not invest, you do not get the return. If you invest inconsistently, you get inconsistent output. If you try to match someone else's returns without matching their deposits, you get injured.

Today, I treat preventive care like a quarterly review. I schedule my annual physical and blood work. I track sleep quality, blood pressure, cholesterol, and energy levels. Not because something is wrong. Because I want to keep things right.

I treat pain and injury as two different signals. One is the cost of growth. The other is a warning. If you do not know the difference, you will either quit too early or push until you break. The CEO move is simple: know when to push—and know when to pivot.

Ignoring signals like tightness, swelling, or chronic fatigue does not make them disappear. It increases the bill later.

That bill has a name: the Pain Tax.

The Pain Tax: The Cost You Always Pay—Either Now or Later

In business, poor decisions do not disappear. They accumulate. They compound. And eventually, they show up on the balance sheet.

Health works the same way.

I call this the Pain Tax.

The Pain Tax is the accumulated cost you pay for ignoring, delaying, or avoiding health decisions you already know you should make. And like any tax, you do not get to opt out. You only get to choose when you pay—and how much.

The cost is not abstract. The CDC estimates that chronic diseases driven by preventable risk factors—poor nutrition, physical inactivity, inadequate sleep, and unmanaged stress—account for more than 75 percent of U.S. healthcare spending and cost American employers over $530 billion annually in lost productivity.[1]

Option 1: Pay the Pain Tax early—in discipline, structure, and preventive investment. Option 2: Pay it later—in disease, medication, diminished capacity, and lost time. Those are the only two options. There is no third.

How the Pain Tax Accumulates

Most people do not wake up unhealthy overnight. Decline happens quietly.

It starts with skipped checkups. Missed workouts. Poor sleep justified by busyness. Convenience eating framed as necessity. Stress left unmanaged because "this is just a busy season."

Each choice feels small. Insignificant. Rational.

But the Pain Tax is not charged daily. It is deferred.

And deferred costs always grow.

What could have been handled with a walk, a routine, or a preventive screening can often turn into blood pressure medication. What could have been managed with boundaries and recovery becomes chronic stress, burnout, or surgery. What could have been corrected with early detection becomes a life-altering diagnosis.

That is not bad luck.

That is accumulated interest.

Reactive Health Is the Most Expensive Strategy

In business, reactive management is the most costly form of leadership. You spend more fixing problems than you ever would have spent preventing them.

Health is no different.

Reactive health looks like this: treating symptoms instead of systems. Paying for prescriptions instead of prevention. Addressing crises instead of trends. Waiting for pain to force action.

Preventive health feels expensive up front because it requires planning, time, and discipline. Reactive health feels cheaper—until the bill comes due.

And when it does, you do not just pay financially. You pay with energy. You pay with mobility. You pay with independence. You pay with time you cannot buy back.

We made a decision years ago: we do not ask "is this expensive?" We ask "what does this return?" That single question reframed every health decision from a cost to a capital allocation.

Our household standard: over-invest in preventive care, under-invest in get-fit-quick programs. Most of our health resources go toward proactive inputs—nutrition, training, recovery, preventive screenings. A smaller reserve handles reactive needs. That balance keeps the enterprise stable.

The Illusion of "Later"

One of the most dangerous words in health is later.

"I'll get back in shape later."

"I'll deal with this after things slow down."

"I'll take it seriously when it gets worse."

That is how the Pain Tax hides.

Later always feels safer than now. But later is where costs explode. Most people do not change because they lack information. They change because the Pain Tax finally becomes unbearable. The diagnosis. The scare. The medication list. The loss of capacity they assumed would never happen to them.

By then, the choices are narrower, the timeline is shorter, and the recovery is harder.

CEOs Don't Ignore Known Liabilities

If you were running a company and knew there was a risk quietly growing in the background—one that would eventually cripple operations—you would not ignore it. You would address it early, while you still had leverage.

Your health deserves the same leadership.

Paying the Pain Tax early looks like scheduling preventive care before symptoms appear. Investing in strength, sleep, and stress management now. Choosing sustainability over shortcuts. Making small, consistent decisions that reduce future exposure.

These are not sacrifices. They are strategic payments that prevent catastrophic loss.

> *You will pay the Pain Tax either way. The only question is whether you pay with discipline now, or with regret later.*

For every dollar invested in preventive wellness programs, research shows a return of $3.27 in reduced medical costs and $2.73 in lower absenteeism.[2] More recent analyses suggest these returns vary by program design and workforce demographics — but the directional finding is consistent across the literature: prevention costs less than treatment. The Pain Tax always costs more than the discipline that avoids it.

LeBron James and the Compounding Return

LeBron James[3] is among the most documented examples of health as strategic capital allocation in professional sports. Over a career spanning more than two decades, he invested heavily across every dimension of physical performance—personal chefs, strength coaches, sleep optimization, and recovery protocols that consumed a significant portion of his annual earnings.

LeBron treats performance capacity as a depreciating asset—one that requires active, systematic investment to hold its value. The principle is not about the dollar amount. It is about treating your physical output as a line item in your operating budget, not an afterthought.

The ROI is documented: a career that outlasted nearly every peer, performed at elite level long past the point where most players decline, and produced results that compounded rather than diminished.

LeBron's strategy makes one executive truth unmistakable: when you treat your health like an undervalued asset, it depreciates fast. When you invest intentionally and consistently, your returns compound.

You are not chasing NBA championships. But the principle is identical. The asset is the same. The compounding logic is the same. What you invest in your health today determines what your health returns to you at 50, 60, 70, and beyond.

Health is not just another budget category. It is the prime asset that determines the output of every other area of your life.

What You Put In Determines What You Get Out

You built the SIS standard in Chapter 3. Here is how it connects to investment thinking—because what you fuel the asset with determines what the asset returns.

Think of your nutrition like the three fuel grades at every gas station.

Fuel Grade	What It Includes	The Real Cost
REGULAR UNLEADED Fast food and processed choices	Burgers, fries, chips, sodas, energy drinks, microwave meals, ingredient-label paragraphs. Gives the illusion of energy — then crashes faster.	Operational cost: inflammation, unstable glucose, constant hunger, low energy. ROI: Negative. You spend a lot for very little return.
MID-GRADE The mixed portfolio	Decent meals mixed with poor choices. Grilled chicken for lunch, takeout all weekend. Protein bars, flavored yogurts, "healthier" snacks. Occasional meal prep, not consistent.	Operational cost: fluctuating energy, unpredictable progress, stalled results. ROI: Neutral. Enough return to feel like you're doing something. Not enough to change performance.
PREMIUM — SIS Strategic, Intentional, Sustainable	Single-ingredient whole foods: chicken, salmon, eggs, sweet potato, oats, vegetables, fruit. Clean proteins. Smart carbs. Healthy fats. Hydration as a daily KPI.	Operational cost: low. Performance return: elite. ROI: Exponential. Engine performs better today and compounds over time.

> *Regular unleaded fuels your cravings. Mid-grade fuels your attempts. Premium fuels your life.*

Most people want premium-fuel performance on regular-fuel habits. They demand high energy, weight loss, focus, strength, and emotional stability while filling the tank with the nutritional equivalent of cheap gasoline.

The quality of your inputs determines the quality of your outputs. That is not a wellness principle. That is operational logic.

SIS in Practice—A Client Story

Several years ago I was coaching a client who swore that eating healthy was "too confusing." He had tried keto, paleo, low-carb, no-carb, juice cleanses, and every program Instagram could sell. Every attempt collapsed. His nutrition system was too complex. Too many rules. Too much decision fatigue.

So I gave him one filter:

"Don't change your calories. Don't change your meal schedule. Just follow one rule. If a food has one ingredient, it's fair game. If it reads like a chemistry quiz, skip it."

He laughed. "That's it?"

Yes. That was it.

Suddenly his choices became obvious.

Chicken is one ingredient.

Broccoli is one ingredient.

Eggs are one ingredient.

Sweet potatoes are one ingredient.

Now look at what was quietly running his weight up: snack bars with 19 ingredients, frozen meals with preservatives he could not pronounce, drinks that had more chemicals than calories.

Within two weeks, the scale moved. Not because he starved himself. Because he finally removed the invisible calories hiding in processed foods.

He was not dieting. He was simplifying.

The one-ingredient rule is the CEO version of nutritional risk mitigation. You remove complexity, eliminate hidden liabilities, and operate from clean data. When your inputs are pure, your outputs improve. Losing weight is not hard when the system is not overloaded. The problem is not discipline. It is complexity.

The SIS Principle—One Rule That Manages the Math for You

Here is the operational mechanism behind why SIS works without counting:

When you follow SIS as your baseline, you naturally stay within a healthy caloric range without tracking a single number. Whole foods are low-calorie but high-volume. You cannot binge on meat, potatoes, fruit, or vegetables the way you can on processed food. The structure of whole food makes overeating physically difficult.

SIS does not ask you to eat less. It asks you to eat real. The volume stays. The hidden liabilities leave. The system runs cleaner.

Your Health Portfolio—Three CEO Moves

Once you accept that health is capital, the question becomes simple: how do you allocate it well?

Three moves. In order.

Move 1: Defund the Liabilities

Every portfolio has dead weight. Assets that are quietly draining performance without delivering return.

In your health portfolio, liabilities look like: convenience food that costs recovery, late-night scrolling that steals sleep, random purchases with no KPI attached, stress spending that substitutes for actual regulation.

This is not exciting. But it is where the money is. If you want a higher-performing portfolio, start by defunding what undermines it.

Move 2: Fund the High-Return Fundamentals

The best health investments are not exotic. They are boring and effective.

Sleep protection. Strength training. Daily movement. Real food. Preventive care. Stress regulation.

Those are the blue-chip stocks in your portfolio. If you are spending on supplements but inconsistent with sleep, your portfolio is upside down. Fund the fundamentals first. Then, and only then, consider upgrades.

Move 3: Buy Execution, Not Information

Most people do not need more knowledge. They need tighter execution. That is why the most valuable health investments are the ones that reduce friction and increase consistency: systems that make healthy eating automatic, coaching that creates accountability and progression, tools that improve recovery so you can stay consistent.

The decision filter is one question:

> *Does this purchase increase my likelihood of executing the fundamentals every week?*

If yes, it is an investment. If no, it is a distraction.

Walking My Wellness Talk—The KPIs That Tell Me the Truth

I do not track everything. Here is what I actually invest in and what I measure to know if it is working.

My five core investments:

- Strength training—my insurance policy for aging well.
- SIS baseline nutrition—not perfect, but consistent. When I drift, I return to the standard.
- Walking—the lowest-friction, highest-ROI habit in my portfolio. Travel, stress, or schedule changes never cancel a walk.
- Sleep discipline—not perfect, but prioritized. When my sleep falls apart, every other KPI reflects the hit.
- Preventive care and bloodwork—I would rather find the story early through data than late through symptoms.

The KPIs that give me the clearest picture:

- HRV (Heart Rate Variability)—my stress dashboard. When it dips, recovery, sleep, or emotional bandwidth needs attention.
- Sleep efficiency—I track depth and consistency more than hours. Good sleep makes everything else easier.
- Resting heart rate—when it rises for more than a few days, my body is waving a yellow flag.
- Glucose stability—the most immediate feedback loop I have

used. In my data, one poor meal or a short night shows up the next morning.

- Training consistency—not PRs, not max lifts. Just: did I show up? Did I move? Did I invest in tomorrow's strength?

These KPIs do not make me obsessive. They make me accountable.

Today, my health portfolio is strong—not perfect, not finished, but strong. My HRV trends higher because I treat recovery as mission-critical. Strength is solid, but mobility still needs more investment. Sleep is good until it is not—I am still working on protecting my bedtime the way I protect my meetings.

This is why I never pretend to have mastered the system. I am still adjusting. Still learning. Still refining. And the more data I collect, the better I understand myself. In EHOS terms, the Three CEO Moves are the investment layer of the Adjust phase—not just correcting what is broken, but actively allocating resources toward what compounds over time.

Your Health ROI Scoreboard

Pick the five to seven KPIs that tell the truth for you. The goal is not to track your life. The goal is to lead your health.

Figure 4.1 *Health Investment ROI — Inputs, KPIs, and Returns*

Investment	KPI (What You Track)	ROI (What You Get)
Strength training	Lifts/progression, consistency	More strength, better posture, injury resilience
Daily walking / conditioning	Steps, minutes, resting heart rate trend	More energy, better stamina, lower long-term risk
Sleep protection	Sleep window consistency, quality score	Better focus, recovery, and mood stability
SIS baseline nutrition	Number of SIS meals/days, waist trend	Stable weight, fewer cravings, cleaner energy
Preventive care	Blood pressure, key labs, screenings completed	Early detection, risk reduction, fewer surprises
Stress downshift rituals	Stress rating (1–5), recovery days honored	Better regulation, less burnout, better decisions

Before you invest in any new program, supplement, coach, or piece of equipment, ask one question: what KPI will this improve? How fast should I expect to see movement? What will I stop doing if I start this? If you cannot answer those questions, it is not a strategy. It is marketing.

1. Run the Health ROI Allocation Audit on Operating Sheet 4.1. Identify your top two leaks. Cut one this month. Redirect that resource toward one high-return fundamental. One reallocation changes the entire portfolio trajectory.
2. Build your Executive Minimalism KPI Dashboard on Operating Sheet 4.2. Pick three inputs, two outputs, and one to two risk indicators. Track them for 30 days. If a KPI is not moving a metric that matters, it is not an investment. It is entertainment.
3. Run your fuel station audit. Look at the last seven days of meals. What grade was most of your fuel? Regular, mid-grade, or premium? Identify one meal per day you will shift to SIS-standard this week. One change. Repeated daily. That is how the portfolio improves.

EXECUTIVE DEBRIEF

Health is capital. The Pain Tax is not avoidable—it is only deferrable, and deferral always adds interest. Think of it like the IRS. The interest does not wait for a convenient time. It does not negotiate with your schedule. It compounds quietly until the bill arrives. The CEO who pays the Pain Tax early pays with discipline. The CEO who delays pays with options they no longer have.

"You will pay the Pain Tax either way. The only question is whether you pay with discipline now, or with regret later."

Health ROI Allocation Audit

Purpose: Identify low-return leaks and reallocate toward one high-return investment. Run this once a month.

CEO Rule: In business you don't find money—you reallocate it. Cut waste. Redirect to what moves the scoreboard. Your health budget works the same way.

Operating Sheet 4.2

Executive Minimalism KPI Dashboard

Purpose: Track what tells the truth. Manage what matters. Pick 5–7 KPIs max and review weekly.

Standard: If you cannot name the KPI, you are not managing the investment. You are guessing. Define the return before you fund the initiative.

CONGRATULATIONS—YOU'VE EARNED THESE SKILLS

Health Capital Allocator—Evaluated and reallocated health investments—time, money, and energy—using ROI criteria to identify high-return priorities and eliminate low-return leaks.

Pain Tax Risk Manager—Identified and addressed known health liabilities proactively, calculating the deferred cost of inaction and converting risk awareness into governed preventive action.

Health KPI Dashboard Designer—Built a personal health performance dashboard tracking leading indicators, output metrics, and early-warning risk signals to lead health decisions with data.

Category	Your Audit
Current Leaks (circle top 2)	Convenience food / delivery Late-night screens → sleep loss Skipped movement due to schedule drift Random purchases (supplements/gear) without KPI impact Stress spending (impulse buys, reactive coping)
Cut One Leak This Month	Leak I'm reducing: ___________________________ How I'll reduce it (specific): ___________________________
Reallocate to One High-Return Investment	Investment I'm funding: ___________________________ Why it pays (one sentence): ___________________________ KPI I'll track: ___________________________ Review cadence: Weekly / Monthly

Category	Your Scoreboard
Inputs (pick 3 — weekly controllables)	1. Sleep window consistency (nights on target): ______ /7 2. Strength sessions completed: ______ /week 3. Daily movement (steps or minutes): ___________________ Optional: SIS baseline meals: ______ /week
Outputs (pick 2 — performance results)	1. Energy consistency (1–5): ______ average 2. Recovery speed / mood stability (1–5): ______ average Optional: Waistline trend: Up / Flat / Down
Risk (pick 1–2 — early warnings)	1. Blood pressure trend: ___________________________ 2. Resting heart rate trend: ___________________________ Optional: Labs review date: ___________________________
Decision Rule	If you can change it this week → it's an Input. If it reflects performance → it's an Output. If it predicts future cost → it's Risk. Track 5–7 KPIs max. The goal is to lead your health, not track your life.

Capital without oversight has one destination. Chapter 5 builds the governance that protects what you just invested.

Chapter Five

Build Your Personal Health Board —

Governance Is What Makes the Plan Survive

No great CEO runs the enterprise alone. Neither should you.

The investment layer is in place. EHOS now shifts into its fourth phase—governance. Because capital without oversight is how enterprises drift.

The best strategy in the world fails when there is no one to protect it. Not because the CEO stops caring. Because the CEO is human—tired, overextended, negotiating with comfort at the end of a hard week. Every high-performing organization has a structure that holds the mission when leadership is under pressure. Your health needs the same.

That structure is your Personal Health Board of Directors.

Not a cheer squad. Not a group chat. Governance—expertise, oversight, accountability, and risk reduction—built to protect the asset when life gets loud.

No Great CEO Goes It Alone

The Devil Wears Prada is one of Tasha's favorite movies. Her favorite moment has nothing to do with the fashion. It is Miranda Priestly, standing completely certain of herself, delivering one line: 'There's no one who can do what I do.'

That confidence is exactly what you should carry about your own health. No one is more equipped to manage, protect, and optimize your body than you are. No specialist, no coach, no program knows your life, your schedule, your history, or your standards better than you do.

But Miranda's fatal leadership flaw is the same one that ends most health plans: she runs everything alone. The confidence is right. The structure around it is missing. You need both—the conviction that no one runs your health better than you, and the board structure that makes sure you never have to run it completely alone.

When Mary Barra stepped into the CEO role at General Motors in January 2014—the first woman to lead a major global automaker—she understood from day one that leadership was not a solo endeavor.

Her first priority was not a product launch. It was not a cost-cutting initiative. It was assembling the right leadership infrastructure around the mission. Barra recognized that sustainable performance demanded more than individual brilliance. It required a carefully built coalition of people with the right expertise, the right authority, and the right mandate to protect the enterprise.[1]

From that lens, the CEO's job is inseparable from the quality of the team around it. Delegation is not weakness. It is how high-performing organizations scale decisions beyond what one person can carry alone.

Your health enterprise works the same way.

Most people fail at health not because they do not care. They fail because their health enterprise has no governance. They make decisions in isolation. They rely on motivation to cover what structure should handle. And when life gets busy, execution collapses under the weight of running everything solo.

Here is the problem, stated plainly:

> *You do not have a health plan issue. You have an oversight issue.*

The most common excuse sounds responsible: I do not have time. But without oversight, health always becomes the first line item that gets cut. A Personal Health Board fixes that—not by cheering louder, but by governing better.

Governance, Not Cheerleading

A real board exists to do five things. Not one of them is making you feel better.

- Reduce risk—catch preventable problems early, before they become expensive.
- Increase decision quality—bring expertise you do not have and perspective you cannot see when you are in it.

63

- Protect execution—make the plan harder to abandon when pressure hits.
- Challenge blind spots—call out the thing you keep rationalizing.
- Hold the CEO accountable—not with shame. With standards.

If you are the CEO of your health, your board's job is simple: protect the asset and protect the mission.

To make this practical, stop thinking about people. Start thinking about seats.

A seat is a role with a purpose. One person can hold more than one seat. Some seats are professional. Some are personal. But every seat must earn its place. And if someone does not reduce risk, improve decisions, or protect execution, they do not get a seat. The CISO seat builds your relapse prevention system—the triggers, boundaries, and contingency plans that stop stress from becoming sabotage. The Culture and Talent seat governs your environment: the people around you, the food defaults at home, and whether the world you live in reinforces or quietly undermines your standards.

Figure 5.1 *Personal Health Board — Seat Map and Qualification Standards*

Seat	Role	Qualification Standard
Chair Governance + Truth	Calls drift early. Protects the mission when you start negotiating with comfort. The person with permission to tell you the truth fastest.	Truth over comfort. Always. Does not need credentials. Needs credibility and backbone. If they only tell you what you want to hear, they are not the Chair.
Chief Medical Advisor Risk + Prevention	Prevention, screenings, labs, and early detection aligned to your real risk profile. Not "doctor when something hurts." Medical oversight before symptoms.	Licensed expertise aligned to your specific risk profile. Prevention mindset, not purely reactive. If they only respond to crises, they are your emergency team, not your board.
COO of Execution Systems + Consistency	Turns intentions into operations. Calendar decisions, defaults, minimum standards, contingency planning. Does not motivate you. Operationalizes you.	Proven ability to build routines that survive real schedules. Designs systems, not programs. Does not sell intensity.

CFO of Health ROI + Capital Allocation	Asks the uncomfortable question: What are we funding and what are we defunding? Prevents upside-down investment.	Clear budgeting discipline and decision filtering. If everything is a health investment, nothing is.
CISO Risk Controls + Relapse Prevention	Builds triggers, boundaries, and contingency plans so stress does not become sabotage. Enforces controls. Calls the breach.	Pattern recognition around your failure triggers. Authority to enforce controls. If they avoid hard conversations, they cannot hold this seat.
Culture & Talent Identity + Environment	Governs your environment: family norms, social patterns, food defaults, and the people around you. Culture eats strategy.	Alignment with the mission. Protects environment standards. Designs celebrations that reinforce identity, not undermine it.

The rule: Your board must make execution easier and drift harder. If someone adds noise, shame, drama, or confusion, they are not a board member. They are a liability.

SECTION 3 — BOARD SEATS HAVE QUALIFICATIONS

You Fill Seats Based on Competence, Not Convenience

This is where most people get it wrong. They confuse support with governance. They build a team of people who make them feel better, not people who make them execute better.

A real board does not exist to be nice. It exists to protect the asset.

There are two categories of board members.

Professional directors—paid expertise. Credentialed. They bring skill, judgment, and pattern recognition you do not have.

Independent directors—trusted truth-tellers. They may not be technical experts, but they protect governance. They call drift early. They challenge blind spots. They do not let you lie to yourself.

Your board needs both. You need expertise. And you need truth.

The Qualification Test

In any serious organization, board members are vetted before they are seated. Not because the process is bureaucratic—because the wrong person in a governance seat does more damage than an empty seat.

For your health board, the vetting is simple. Three questions for every candidate:

Do they have real expertise or lived experience in this domain—a degree, a certification, a track record you can verify? Opinion is not a qualification.

Are they currently practicing what they would govern? A former athlete who has not trained in ten years does not hold the same seat as someone actively in the work.

Can they tell you the truth when comfort is easier? Past expertise means nothing if the person cannot challenge you when you need it most.

Every seat on your board should pass all three. If someone clears two out of three, they are a resource—not a board member.

Before You Give Anyone a Seat—Run These Questions

- Do they have proven expertise in the seat they are holding?
- Do they tell the truth, or do they tell me what I want to hear?
- Do they improve decision quality, or create more confusion?
- Do they respect sustainability over intensity?
- Will they help me execute when life gets loud?

If the answer is no, do not seat them. This is your health enterprise. You are not building a social circle. You are building governance.

My Chair: The Governance Standard in Real Life

A board is only as effective as its governance. And governance only works when there is a Chair who has the backbone to call the meeting when drift shows up.

Not a mascot. Not a motivational speaker. A Chair.

For my Health Board, my wife Tasha is my Chair.

Not because she is nicer than everyone else. Because she has the biggest long-term investment in my health. We are building a life together. That means my energy, my mobility, and my longevity are not personal goals. They are shared assets. The same is true in reverse. We both have equity in this enterprise.

When one of us breaks down, the other pays—in time, stress, options, and freedom. That is the hidden cost most couples never price in.

Our goal is simple to say and hard to execute: we want our healthspan to match our lifespan. We have seen too many couples get more years but fewer good ones. The lifespan keeps extending while the healthspan quietly shrinks. We are not naive about what we can and cannot prevent. But we take every precaution we can to improve the odds.

That is what makes Tasha the Chair. She does not let me negotiate with comfort in the moment if it threatens the long-term plan. She protects the asset because she understands the return—not just for me, but for us.

Sometimes I think I am making a logical decision. She asks one question and exposes the real reason.

> *"Are you making a strategic choice—or are you negotiating with comfort?"*

That is Chair behavior.

And then there is the morning crew. None more consistent than Delvin—who has shown up alongside me for over 25 years through every season, every setback, and every early morning that required more discipline than motivation. That kind of long-term accountability is not a friendship courtesy. It is a governance asset.

Every morning, I lead a group workout before the day starts. That crew is not just accountability—it is an advisory council. Their dedication is my execution engine. Their energy sets the standard. Their presence makes discipline non-negotiable in a way that solo effort never can. Before 7:00 a.m., I have already had spiritual grounding, mental clarity, emotional release, and a training session. That is what the right board does. It provides—before you even ask—what most people would have to hire individually.

When the Chair Seat Fails—A Client Story

I once had a client—I will not use her name, but if she is reading this, she knows exactly who she is.

She made her husband the Chair of her Health Board.

Big mistake.

Not because he did not love her. Because he loved peace more than truth. His governance style was simple: approve everything. She would exercise when she felt like it. Eat what she wanted. Skip the plan. Ignore the standards. And he would sign off on all of it like he was the Board Chair of Denial, Inc.

When I found out what was happening, I told her directly: "You need to fire him."

Not from your life. From the seat.

Because a Chair who only tells you what you want to hear is not a Chair. That is a hype-man with veto power.

Here is what made it worse. Eventually, he did try to tell the truth. He finally attempted accountability. And because there was no governance agreement, no decision rights, and no shared standard, it did not land as leadership. It landed as betrayal. It took a lot of conversations—and yes, counseling—to recover from what should have been a simple health correction.

Chair Qualification Rule: Truth over comfort. Always.

Decision Rights Rule: If expectations are not explicit, accountability feels like betrayal.

Risk First. Execution Second. Performance Third.

Most people build their health team backwards. They start with what feels exciting: a new program, a challenge, a supplement stack, a gadget.

That is not leadership. That is shopping.

Real executives build governance in the correct sequence.

Step 1: Fill the Risk Seats First

If you do not reduce risk early, you end up funding problems later. Start with the two seats that protect the enterprise from preventable downside.

Chief Medical Advisor—prevention, screenings, labs, and early detection aligned to your real risk profile. Not the doctor you see when something hurts. The advisor who monitors before symptoms appear.

Chair—your governance anchor. The seat you filled in Section 2.

If you build nothing else, build these two. The biggest failures in health are rarely surprise attacks. They are unreviewed trends and ignored signals.

Step 2: Install Execution Support

Once risk is covered, build consistency. The COO of Execution is the seat that turns your intentions into operations: calendar decisions, default routines, minimum viable standards, and contingency planning when life gets loud. This seat does not motivate you. It operationalizes you.

Step 3: Add ROI Discipline

The CFO seat asks the uncomfortable question: what are we funding—and what are we defunding? Many people spend real money on "health" while chronically underfunding fundamentals like sleep, nutrition infrastructure, and preventive care. A CFO does not let the enterprise go upside down. Neither should you.

Step 4: Add Controls

In cybersecurity, the breach is rarely because someone stopped caring. It is because controls were weak and enforcement was inconsistent. Your health derails the same way—travel, stress, late nights, emotional eating, missed workouts compounding into missed weeks. The CISO seat builds relapse prevention: trigger identification, boundary enforcement, and re-entry rules for when drift happens. After 30 years in corporate cybersecurity, I know that breaches are not random. They are patterned. Your health relapses work the same way—predictable triggers, weak enforcement, and no pre-written response. The CISO seat closes that gap.

The Interim Rule

You may not have the perfect board today. That is fine. Companies run interim leaders all the time—someone holds the seat while the right long-term person is identified. Health is no different.

But if you fill a seat yourself—Chair, CFO discipline, Culture—you still have to operate like a qualified board member. Tell yourself the truth. Enforce decision rights. Keep the cadence. Protect the non-negotiables when life gets loud.

Interim is allowed. Unqualified is not.

A Board That Does Not Meet Is Not a Board. It's a Concept.

The board charter is how you turn good intentions into governance. Before you invite anyone into a seat, you set the operating agreement.

- Mission: what are we protecting? Energy. Longevity. Capability.
- Non-negotiables: the standards the Chair protects when life gets messy.
- Decision rights: who advises, who approves, who is accountable.

If everyone has an opinion but no one has authority, you get noise, not governance.

- Cadence: boards do not meet when things get bad. They meet on rhythm.

Here is the board meeting structure that works. Simple. Repeatable. Real.

Figure 5.2 *Board Review Cadence — Weekly, Monthly, Quarterly*

Cadence	Questions to Run
Weekly — 10 minutes Operations Check	What drifted this week? What is the single highest-leverage correction? What is my minimum standard on my worst day?
Monthly — 20 minutes Strategy Review	Are my KPIs trending the right direction? What is costing me the most energy right now? What needs to be funded or defunded?
Quarterly — 30 minutes Portfolio Audit	What is working that we should double down on? What is not working that we should cut? What risk needs attention before it gets expensive?

You can be the CEO and still need governance. That is not weakness. That is how high performers stay high performing. The enterprise does not collapse when you stop caring. It collapses when you stop reviewing. The Chair makes sure you do not. In EHOS terms, your board governance structure is the Review phase made permanent—the cadence that ensures Assess → Review → Adjust → Repeat never stops running regardless of what else is happening in your life.

THREE ACTION STEPS

1. Fill the two risk seats this week. Name your Chair and your Chief Medical Advisor. Write them down on Operating Sheet 5. These are not aspirational selections—they are governance decisions. If you cannot name them today, identify the gap and set a date to fill it.
2. Write your Board Charter on Operating Sheet 5. Three non-negotiables. One cadence. Decision rights assigned. This takes ten minutes and converts your health plan from a perosonal commitment into a governed enterprise.

3. Schedule your first Weekly Executive Review this week. Same day. Same time. Ten minutes. Three questions. If it is not on the calendar, it is not real. A board that does not meet is just a concept.

EXECUTIVE DEBRIEF

The board exists to protect the enterprise when you are tired, overextended, or negotiating with comfort. The seat map gives you roles with standards. The credential ladder gives you a qualification system instead of a preference list. The Chair keeps you honest when honesty is inconvenient.

*"The enterprise does not collapse when you stop caring.
It collapses when you stop reviewing."*

OPERATING SHEET 5—YOUR HEALTH BOARD

Complete this Operating Sheet in the book, or log your answers directly into the EHOS Dashboard at adrianmwilliams.com. Members with a free account can access all worksheets, save their responses by chapter, and generate their CEO of Me Health Resume automatically from their answers.

Executive Action 1—Fill the Two Risk Seats: Name your Chair and your Chief Medical Advisor. Write them down. These are governance decisions, not aspirational selections. If you cannot name them today, set a date to fill the gap.

Executive Action 2—Write Your Board Charter: Three non-negotiables. One cadence. Decision rights assigned. Ten minutes. This converts your health plan from a personal commitment into a governed enterprise.

Executive Action 3—Schedule Your First Weekly Executive Review: Same day. Same time. Ten minutes. Three questions. If it is not on the calendar, it is not real.

Health Board Architect—Assembled a Personal Health Board of Directors with defined seat qualifications, role-specific expertise requirements, and accountability structures that provide governance beyond what any individual can self-supply.

Health Oversight Manager—Established weekly, monthly, and quarterly board review rhythms, converting health governance from an intention into a structured recurring cadence with defined questions, decision rights, and accountability checkpoints.

Health Governance Specialist—Defined board member roles, non-negotiable standards, and accountability structures that protect the health operating system from drift, emotion-driven decisions, and the erosion that follows unreviewed momentum.

The structure holds on a good week. Chapter 6 is the stress test.

Figure 5.3 *Board Roster — Seat Status Tracker*

Seat	Name / Status
Chair Governance + Truth	Name: ________________________________ Qualification confirmed: Yes / Interim / TBD
Chief Medical Advisor Risk + Prevention	Name: ________________________________ Specialty aligned to my risk profile: __________
COO of Execution Systems + Consistency	Name: ________________________________ Qualification confirmed: Yes / Interim / TBD
CFO of Health ROI + Allocation	Name: ________________________________ Qualification confirmed: Yes / Interim / TBD
CISO Controls + Relapse Prevention	Name: ________________________________ Qualification confirmed: Yes / Interim / TBD
Culture & Talent Environment + Identity	Name: ________________________________ Qualification confirmed: Yes / Interim / TBD
Rule	Interim is allowed. Unqualified is not. If a seat is empty, name the gap and set a fill date.

Charter Element	Your Answer
Mission (what are we protecting?)	Energy / Longevity / Capability Other: ____
Non-Negotiables (standards we enforce)	1. ____ 2. ____ 3. ____
Decision Rights	Chair has permission to call drift early: Yes / No Who approves medical escalation? ________________ Who owns execution scheduling? _________________ Who enforces relapse controls? _________________
Cadence	Weekly Executive Review (10 min): Day/Time ______ Monthly Strategy Review (20 min): Day/Time ______ Quarterly Portfolio Audit (30 min): Month ________
Interim Seat Rule	Interim is allowed. Unqualified is not. Interim holder: _________________________________ Timeline to fill permanently: ___________________

See Figure 5.2 — Board Review Cadence (page reference above).

No review means no leadership. If it is not on the calendar, it is not real.

CHAPTER SIX

Sustaining the Turnaround —
Build a System That Survives the Week You Didn't Plan For

Anyone can execute a great plan on a great week. The CEO move is executing when nothing goes your way.

Not by your best week. By your worst one. The week where three things go sideways at once, where motivation is nowhere to be found, where the plan meets reality and one of them has to give.

Most health plans do not fail at the strategy level. They fail at the sustainability level. The plan was built for a perfect week. Life delivered a real one.

This chapter is how you build a system that holds regardless of which week shows up. This is where EHOS stress-tests itself—the Adjust phase under real-world pressure, not ideal conditions.

A Pitch Is What You Say You Will Do. An Operation Is What You Can Repeat Under Pressure.

One of my favorite shows has always been Shark Tank. After all these seasons, the pattern is clear. You know what works. You know what the Sharks invest in and what they shut down fast.

And you know this: data and numbers matter. Confidence does not close deals. Capacity does.

Picture the entrepreneur walking through those doors—adrenaline high, lights blazing, Sharks staring. The pitch starts strong.

"I'm asking for $200,000 for 10 percent."

Then the pitch machine turns on.

"If we capture just 1 percent of the market..."
"If we get into Target..."
"If we do a million in year one..."
For a moment, the dream sounds inevitable.

But the Sharks are not there to fund dreams. They are there to test sustainability. Because everyone in that room knows the difference between a pitch and an operation.

So the questions come fast.

"What are your sales right now?"
"What are your margins?"
"What breaks first when demand spikes?"
Shark Tank is not a show about confidence. It is a show about capacity.

Health is no different.

Most people do not build a sustainable health strategy. They build a health pitch.

"I'm going to work out six days a week."
"I'm cutting out sugar starting Monday."
"I'm going to overhaul my sleep, my diet, and my stress—all at once, next quarter, when things slow down."
That is the "1 percent of the market" line in health form. It sounds bold. It feels good. It looks great in your head.

Then the real questions show up.

What happens when you travel? When work gets heavy? When you sleep four hours and your stress is high and your discipline is low? When the kids get sick and you are the only one who can leave to get them? When soccer practice runs late and dinner was never planned? When your calendar collapses at 2 p.m. and the evening you designed on Sunday no longer exists? When the week looks nothing like the one you planned for? That is the week this system was built for.

That is the sustainability test. And most plans fail right there—because they were built for an ideal calendar instead of a real one.

Sustainable health is not about having a bigger goal. It is about having a system that survives the week you did not plan for. That is what the Sharks fund. Not the pitch—the capacity to stay in business. Most people design their health plan for their best-case schedule and try to execute it through their real one. That pattern has a name. Chapter 9 gives it one.

The Obstacle Removal Protocol

When execution breaks down, most people look inward. They decide they lack willpower, discipline, or motivation.

That diagnosis is almost always wrong.

Obstacles are not character flaws. They are friction points. And friction points can be engineered out of the system.

Your board is a resource here. From your Chair to your COO of Execution, the people in your governance structure exist precisely to help you manage disruption before it becomes drift. Use them. Do not try to problem-solve in isolation what your board was built to handle together.

The most common obstacles are not mysteries:

- Time—the calendar does not have room for the full plan.
- Energy—the tank is too low to execute at full capacity.
- Environment—the defaults around you pull toward the wrong choice.
- Social pressure—the people around you normalize lower standards.
- Motivation—the feeling is gone and the system is not strong enough to run without it.

Each of those is a system problem with a system solution. Here is the tool:

The Obstacle Removal Protocol (ORP)

Run this in under ten minutes when execution starts breaking down. Do not wait until you have fully drifted. Run it at the first sign of friction. In

EHOS terms, the ORP is the Adjust step made actionable—not a vague intention to do better, but a five-minute diagnostic that produces one specific change.

Figure 6.1 *Obstacle Removal Protocol (ORP) — Five-Step Framework*

ORP Step	Your Answer
1. Name the obstacle (one sentence)	What is making execution break down right now?
2. Find the friction (what makes it hard?)	What is the specific barrier?
3. Remove one barrier (make it easier)	Reduce time: _______________ Reduce steps: _______________ Reduce decisions: _______________ Reduce temptation: _______________
4. Install a minimum standard (what still counts?)	The smallest version that keeps the system alive:
5. Assign accountability (board check)	Who on my Health Board will check this — and when?
Reminder	Turnarounds do not fail from lack of knowledge. They fail from unmanaged friction.

Turnarounds do not fail from lack of knowledge. They fail from unmanaged friction.

The power to overcome obstacles does not come without mental resilience. My inherent competitiveness—fostered by my sisters' childhood taunts of 'I dare you' and 'I bet you can't'—continues to motivate me today. Mom, sorry again for all those hospital visits.

Setting incremental, achievable goals consistently fuels that drive. Whether increasing push-up reps or hitting weightlifting milestones, each small victory builds the discipline to keep going—even when immediate results are not apparent. That is not motivation. That is a system that has been running since childhood.

Milestones Are Reinforcement, Not Finish Lines

You have heard the line: life is too short not to celebrate the good moments. True. But here is the CEO version:

> *Celebration is not the finish line. Celebration is reinforcement.*

Every milestone matters. Big wins. Small wins. The week you finally stop drifting. The month you prove you can execute without drama. Those wins are proof of effort, resilience, and growth.

But celebration has a trap. It can turn into a parking lot.

The biggest mistake I see: people hit a goal and start believing they "have it under control." They beat the weight-loss target or fix the thing that scared them—then they get overconfident. Standards soften. Structure slips. And drift quietly returns. I call this the Victory Debt—the drift window that opens every time you win. Chapter 9 builds the full protocol for closing it.

A Personal Example: The Bench Press Target

I set a goal to increase my bench press at 225 pounds—9 reps when I started, with three months to push it as far as I could. The target was 20. I hit 19, and I was fine with that. The goal was never just the number. It was to see what I could get to, give it everything within the window I committed to, and then set the next challenge. That is what keeps the standard rising—not obsessing over what you missed, but immediately locking in what comes next.

When the three months were up, I moved on. Not because I gave up on 20. Because the system requires it. You define the goal, you define the window, you execute, and then you reset. The next challenge starts from where you landed—which is always further than where you began.

Stagnation is celebration's worst enemy.

A Milestone That Mattered More Than a Number

The finish line at the Cherry Blossom 10-Miler told a different story than the clock. The official time was 1:53:09. An 11:18 pace. Not a headline number. But I ran track in high school. I knew what a real running pace felt like. And I knew what it meant to finish that race after rupturing my Achilles and learning to walk again. That finish line was not about the time. It was about the return.

That is why you celebrate. Not to post. Not to perform. Not to pause. To reinforce the message your system needs to hear:

This matters. Keep going.

And even if your win is walking 20 minutes a day for a week, celebrate it. Small wins build emotional momentum. Over time, consistency becomes pride—and pride becomes fuel.

Here is how Tasha and I handle it. For me, celebration usually means gear that improves execution—a 40-pound weight vest, a new recovery tool, something that makes the next chapter better. For Tasha, celebration usually means retail therapy—and honestly, she never needs much of an excuse. The method does not matter. The rule does:

Celebrate + Reset. Celebrate in a way that supports the mission. Then immediately set the next target so progress stays in motion.

The 3-Try Rule—Stop Quitting Too Early

Most people do not fail because the plan is wrong. They fail because they quit too early—or they keep switching plans until nothing sticks.

They try something once. It feels awkward. Results are not immediate. And they label it "not for me."

That is not leadership. That is impatience wearing a suit.

In business, you do not cancel a strategy after the first bad meeting. You run the pilot long enough to tell the truth.

Here is the standard I use for myself and every client: the 3-Try Rule.

Try #1—Exposure: You are learning the mechanics. Expect friction. Do not evaluate outcomes yet.

Try #2—Adjustment: You remove what is unnecessary and reduce the friction. You make it executable.

Try #3—Decision: You decide if it belongs in your operating system. Keep it, modify it, or kill it—based on reality, not emotion.

The Hot Yoga Test

I use this rule on myself.

I tried hot yoga once and hated it—because I hate working out in the heat. It was so hot I started wondering why they keep you in there, then I found out it's for safety in case somebody passes out. I was not enlightened. I was irritated.

I tried it a second time and hated it again—because it was still too hot to concentrate on anything that mattered. I could not focus on stretching. I could not touch my toes. And my downward dog looked less like a yoga pose and more like a dead dog.

Plenty of people love hot yoga. It works for them. The 3-Try Rule is not about judging what others do—it is about knowing what works for your system.

You need enough reps to separate "this is new" from "this does not work for my life." One rep is a reaction. Three reps is a decision.

> *You do not need a new plan. You need enough reps to tell the truth.*

Boredom Is the Silent Assassin of Sustained Discipline

Burnout does not usually show up as quitting. It shows up as drifting.

You get bored. You get stale. You start negotiating with the plan. Then you tell yourself a story: "I'll get back to it when life calms down."

That is not a time problem. That is a sustainability problem.

The answer is not chaos. The answer is strategic variety—small, intentional changes that keep you engaged while still serving the mission.

Grit Without Rotation Is a Setup

I learned this the hard way. When I trained for the Guinness World Record for the most push-ups in an hour, my program was a single movement executed at extreme volume for eight consecutive months. No rotation. No variety. Pure, monotonous repetition. Eight months of the same movement, zero rotation, maximum volume—I did not just ignore strategic variety. I eliminated it entirely. And the system broke before the goal arrived.

The training produced the result the volume would predict: overuse breakdown. On attempt day, I pushed through without knowing I had torn my rotator cuff. I finished with just under 1,200 push-ups. The record didn't fall. I didn't find out about the shoulder until after. The lesson was not about the shoulder. It was about what happens when grit replaces design. Sustained effort without strategic variety does not build a stronger system. It builds a more expensive failure.

Strategic variety is not novelty. It is resilience engineering—building a system that holds up longer because it does not demand the same thing every single day.

Small shifts rekindle engagement without breaking standards:

- Swap a gym session for a hike or outdoor conditioning.
- Try a new cuisine that still meets SIS standard.

- Rotate a recovery method—cold therapy, yoga, mobility work.
- Change the time or location of a training session, not the standard.

The guardrail: variety supports the goal. Distraction replaces the goal. The standard does not change. The method rotates.

Stay in Motion Without Burning Out

Most people do not fail because they do not know what to do. They fail because the plan has no built-in recovery mechanism—no way to re-enter after a miss without declaring the whole thing a failure.

The fix is not more motivation. It is a loop—small, repeatable, and built for real life.

Figure 6.2 *Minimum Viable Day — Seasonal Adjustment Protocol*

Step	What It Means
1 — Plan (night before)	Decide what success looks like tomorrow in one sentence. No morning negotiations. No improvising. Your future self needs a clear roadmap, not a blank calendar.
2 — Execute (minimum standard)	Run the smallest version that still counts. Your plan must survive your worst week, not your best. If it only works when conditions are perfect, it is not a plan.
3 — Track (one metric only)	Pick one metric that proves execution happened. Steps. Workout. SIS meals. Sleep window. If tracking becomes the job, you will quit the job.
4 — Review (Weekly Executive Review)	10 minutes. Three questions: What drifted? What is the single correction that fixes the most? What is my minimum standard on my worst day?
5 — Adjust (one change only)	One upgrade. One friction removed. One standard tightened. Then run the loop again. You do not start over. You re-enter.

Here is what this loop prevents: the emotional roller coaster. You do not start over. You re-enter. You do not guess. You diagnose. You do not spiral. You execute.

Missing once is a data point. Missing twice is a trend. The loop catches the trend before it becomes the default.

Design Your Environment Before It Designs You

The fastest way to undermine a strong plan is to leave the environment unmanaged.

If everyone around you normalizes low standards, your standards will feel extreme. And that is how drift becomes the new normal—not because you stopped caring, but because the environment quietly rewrote the policy.

The Environment Audit

Run this three-question audit when you notice your standards are slipping and you cannot identify why:

1. Who reinforces my standards? People who normalize sleep, movement, real food, and follow-through.
2. Who erodes my standards? People who normalize "we deserve it" as a lifestyle, not an exception.
3. Where do I keep taking avoidable hits? Events, routines, and settings where my default becomes drift.

Your goal is not to cut people off. Your goal is to stop letting unmanaged environments write your policy.

You do not need a dramatic announcement. You need quiet replacement: swap one dine-out for a walk or active hangout. Create traditions that reinforce your mission instead of testing it. Put yourself in rooms where your standards are normal. Because the fastest way to level up your health execution is to level up your default environment.

Occasion Governance

One rule we govern by in our household: we do not let celebrations become self-sabotage rituals.

Birthdays, holidays, promotions, and just-because moments used to come with the same default package: over-ordering at dinner and waking up the next day farther from the mission. Now we govern occasions the same way we govern everything else: with standards.

We still celebrate. We just do not celebrate by damaging the asset.

Our rule: we plan the occasion so it fits the mission—not the other way around. That might mean choosing the restaurant intentionally, ordering with purpose, taking a walk after, or making the experience the celebration instead of the excess. Because if every joyful moment pulls you away from your standards, your standards will not survive a joyful life.

External support is not fluff. It is infrastructure. And when your ecosystem supports your mission, you stop relying on willpower and start relying on design.

Three Action Steps

1. Write your Minimum Standard for this week before this chapter ends. One sentence. Movement minimum, nutrition minimum, recovery minimum. This is not your goal—it is your floor. The smallest version of execution that keeps the system alive when everything else is chaotic. Use Operating Sheet 6.

2. Identify your number one current obstacle and run the Obstacle Removal Protocol on Operating Sheet 6. Name it. Find the friction. Remove one barrier. Assign accountability to your board. Five minutes. Do it before this week ends.

3. Name one habit you have already quit and apply the 3-Try Rule before you write it off permanently. Pick your re-entry date for Try #1. Write it down on Operating Sheet 6 before you close this chapter. A decision made after one attempt is a reaction. A decision made after three is a verdict.

One of our guilty pleasures is brunch at Sequoia's in Georgetown. And trust me, it is no joke. That place is engineered for drift. The smell hits you first. Then the options. Then the slow, casual rhythm that makes a third plate feel normal.

So we do not treat it like a surprise. We treat it like a known risk.

If we know we are going, we plan the day around it. Not with guilt. With design.

We knock out 5 to 6 miles in the morning. Sometimes we add a quick 20 to 30 minute workout. Not because we are trying to "earn" food, but because we are setting the tone. We are reinforcing the identity we want to live in before we step into an environment that tries to rewrite it.

Then we make small decisions that keep the occasion inside the mission. We do not show up starving. We decide the standard before we sit down. We slow down on purpose. We treat the experience as the celebration, not the excess.

That one tradition taught me something simple. The environment always has a plan for you. Music, pace, portions, other people's energy, the unspoken permission to "just enjoy yourself" like your body is not part of your real life.

When we plan Sequoia's, we are not being rigid. We are being governed.

Because unmanaged environments do not just tempt you. They normalize new policies. And if you let that happen often enough, drift stops feeling like drift. It starts feeling like your baseline.

We still celebrate. We just refuse to let a celebration become a recurring self-sabotage ritual.

"If your health plan only works when life is calm, it is not a plan.
It is a performance."

Executive Action 1—Your Minimum Standard: This is your Minimum Viable Day from Chapter 3—made permanent. The floor you execute on your worst week. One sentence. Non-negotiable. My Minimum Standard this week: _________________ Movement minimum: _________________ Nutrition minimum: _________________ Recovery minimum: _________________ Adrian's example: Three 20-minute sessions, one SIS baseline meal per day, screens down by 10 p.m.

Executive Action 2—Your Obstacle Removal: Run this when execution breaks down. Five minutes. The obstacle: _________________ The friction point: _________________ One barrier I will remove: _________________ Board member I will assign: _________________

Executive Action 3—Your 3-Try Commitment: One habit you have already quit. Give it three real reps before deciding. The habit: _________________ Try #1 (when): _________________ Try #2 (friction I will remove): _________________ Try #3 (decision date): _________________

Complete this Operating Sheet in the book, or log your answers directly into the EHOS Dashboard at adrianmwilliams.com. Members with a free account can access all worksheets, save their responses by chapter, and generate their CEO of Me Health Resume automatically from their answers.

Health Resilience Operator—Deployed real-time operational tools—obstacle removal, strategic variety, and environment governance—to sustain health execution through disrupted weeks without losing the system.

Obstacle Removal Specialist—Applied a structured friction-identification and removal protocol to convert execution breakdowns from personal failures into solvable system problems with pre-decided solutions.

Health Environment Architect—Audited and restructured default environmental settings and social occasion protocols to reduce friction and reinforce mission-aligned defaults without relying on willpower.

Element	Your Answer
My Minimum Standard (this season — one sentence)	___________________________________ ___________________________________
Seasonal KPI Focus (one KPI to lead this season)	Training Sessions / Steps-Movement / Sleep Window / SIS Meals / Stress Downshift Why this KPI matters right now: _______________
Non-Negotiable Rules	If I can't do the full plan, I do the minimum plan. Missing once is a data point. Missing twice is a trend. I do not start over. I re-enter.
Examples (pick one that fits)	Training: "3 sessions this week — 20 minutes counts." Movement: "8,000 steps 4 days this week." Nutrition: "SIS breakfast + SIS lunch 5 days this week." Sleep: "Lights out by ______ at least 4 nights."

The system is running. Chapter 7 is where you stop maintaining and start compounding.

Board member assigned: _______________________________________

My minimum standard: _______________________________________

One barrier I will remove: _______________________________________

The friction point: _______________________________________

The obstacle: _______________________________________

Run the ORP (Figure 6.1) on your current obstacle:

Try	Your Plan
Try #1 — Exposure (learn the mechanics)	What exactly will I do? _______________________ Expect friction. Do not evaluate outcomes yet.
Try #2 — Adjustment (reduce friction)	What friction will I remove to make it executable? _______________________
Try #3 — Decision (based on reality, not emotion)	After three reps, I will: Keep it / Modify it / Kill it Reason: _______________________
CEO Rule	If it cannot survive Try #3 in real life, it does not belong in the operating system.

Element	Your Answer
Where am I getting bored? (circle one)	Training / Food / Recovery / Sleep / Tracking
One strategic swap I will run this week	_______________________
What stays the same (my standard)	_______________________
What success looks like (one sentence)	_______________________
Guardrail	Variety supports the goal. Distraction replaces the goal. The standard does not change. The method rotates.

Innovation—Signal Over Noise

Upgrade the System. Never Chase the Trend.

If the upgrade does not change a decision, it is noise. If it changes execution, it is infrastructure.

Chapter 7 asks the next question: once the system is running, how do you make it better?

Innovation in health is not about chasing the newest device, the latest protocol, or the biohack making the rounds on social media. It is about applying the same precision that drives elite performance in every other domain to the system you are already running. Small upgrades. Controlled experiments. Data that changes decisions.

That is the standard. Anything below it is entertainment.

Innovation Without Chaos—The F1 Standard

My wife and I are Formula 1 fans—but not for the reasons most people expect. We are not watching for the crashes or the podium drama. We are watching the innovation. Specifically, we are watching what happens in the 2.4 seconds it takes a pit crew to change four tires, adjust the car, and send a driver back into a race at 200 miles per hour.

It is not just about speed. What impressed us most was the precision of the pit crews, the elite fitness of the drivers, the real-time data influencing every decision mid-race, and the pre-race protocols the team runs like clockwork. F1 does not just race. It reinvents—constantly. Victory is not raw horsepower. It is strategy, adaptability, and continuous improvement applied with discipline.

That insight reframed how I think about health innovation.

An F1 team does not change everything after every race. It changes the right thing—the variable that is actually limiting performance. The engineers review the data, identify the highest-leverage adjustment, test it, measure it, and either keep it or cut it. One change at a time. Controlled. Evidence-based.

Most people do the opposite with health. They change everything at once when nothing is working, then revert to old defaults two weeks later. That is not innovation. That is panic disguised as effort.

The F1 standard applied to EHOS: every upgrade must reduce friction, improve adherence, or reveal a signal you can act on. If it does not do at least one of those three things, it does not make the car faster. It makes the garage more cluttered.

The Background Update

Here is a concept that reframes how you think about health upgrades—and it comes from something you interact with every day. Your phone gives you a choice: update now in small increments, or ignore the notifications until the system slows down, the apps start crashing, and you have no option left but a full reinstall. Most people choose the second option. They dismiss the update, keep running on an outdated system, and then wonder why everything feels harder than it should. A few people set it to auto-update—small patches, in the background, compounding quietly. They never notice the updates. They just notice the system keeps running.

Your phone does not wait until it crashes to update. It updates constantly—small patches, in the background, without drama. You barely notice them. You just notice the system running cleaner, the battery lasting longer, the performance holding up under load.

Most people treat their health the opposite way. They wait until something breaks—a diagnosis, a scare, a medication conversation, the moment the Pain Tax becomes undeniable—and then they do a full system reinstall. New diet. New program. New everything, all at once. That is not innovation. That is emergency maintenance.

The CEO move is the Background Update: small, consistent, invisible when they work. One nutrition adjustment per quarter. One recovery ritual added to the morning routine. One measurement that surfaces a trend before it becomes a problem. You barely notice the update. You just notice the system running better six months from now.

Small. Consistent. Compounding. That is the only system that survives long enough to matter.

The EHOS Innovation Standard—Signal Over Noise

Most people do not quit their health plan because they hate the work. They quit because they get exhausted deciding: What should I do today? Am I doing enough? Is this working? Did I track it right?

Decision fatigue turns good intentions into inconsistency. The fix is not more information. It is a tighter filter.

Before you buy, subscribe, download, or adopt anyone else's routine, run this test:

1. What decision will this improve? Be specific: sleep, training, food, recovery, or risk.
2. What friction will this remove? Planning, tracking, guessing, or inconsistency.
3. What truth will it reveal that you can act on? One signal. One sentence.

If you cannot answer all three in plain language, do not fund it.

One hard truth: *people buy devices they do not use. That is not a technology problem. That is a governance problem. If the tool is not used consistently, it becomes clutter. Clutter becomes avoidance. Avoidance becomes the Pain Tax.*

SECTION 3—KPI DISCIPLINE: THE NUMBER THAT TELLS THE TRUTH

One Primary KPI. Small Supporting Set. Execute.

All KPIs matter. But if you are running an enterprise, you need one primary KPI—the scoreboard you do not negotiate with.

Keep it simple:

> *Consistent progress = commitments kept.*

Not perfection. Not intensity. Commitments kept, week after week. That is the scoreboard. The right primary KPI is the one you cannot talk your way out of.

You do not need five dashboards. You need one primary KPI plus a small supporting set that explains why the scoreboard is moving.

Figure 7.1 *KPI Tier System — Primary and Supporting Metrics*

KPI Tier	What to Track	Options
Primary KPI (pick 1 — your scoreboard)	The one number you cannot negotiate with. Tracks weekly. Consistent progress = commitments kept.	Training sessions completed Sleep window protected (nights/week) SIS baseline meals (per week) Movement minutes or steps (weekly)
Supporting KPIs (pick 2–4 — the drivers)	The inputs that explain why your primary KPI moves. Track weekly.	Protein-first breakfast (days/week) Afternoon crash avoided (days/week) Strength sessions (days/week) Bedtime window hit (days/week) Water target hit (days/week)
Risk KPI (pick 1 — early warning)	The lagging indicator that predicts future cost. Review monthly or quarterly.	Weight trend (weekly average) Waistline trend (monthly) Blood pressure trend (monthly) Annual physical + labs
Signal vs. Noise Rules	If it does not change a decision, it is noise. If tracking becomes the job, you will quit the job. One scoreboard. Small driver set. Execute.	

The Diagnostic First Rule

When you take your car to a mechanic, the first thing they do is plug in the diagnostic reader. They do not guess. They do not open the hood based on instinct. They pull the codes. The codes tell them exactly what is wrong. Then—and only then—do they fix what the data reveals.

Most people innovate their health backwards. They buy the solution before they understand the problem.

- New supplement before bloodwork.
- New training program before understanding their recovery patterns.

- New diet before understanding their glucose response.
- New wearable before knowing which signal actually matters.

That is guessing with good intentions. The results are unpredictable because the diagnosis never happened.

> *A mechanic does not open the hood and start replacing parts. They pull the codes first. Your health innovation should work the same way.*

I call this the Diagnostic First Rule: every meaningful health upgrade starts with a signal. Data before prescription. Diagnosis before solution. The tool is only as smart as the question it is answering.

Here is what that looks like in real life.

Tina's Turning Point—When Data Told the Truth

Tina was six months into being a new mom—a fully remote project manager running global workflows with a baby monitor in one hand and a laptop in the other. Her days were a blur of feedings, deadlines, Slack pings, and stolen sleep. She was not complaining. She loved her baby, she loved her work, and she loved the idea that she could do both.

But her body was not loving any of it.

Every morning she stepped on the scale hoping to see progress. Every morning it greeted her with the same stubborn number. She was not eating junk. She was not cheating. She genuinely believed she was doing everything right. Yogurt bowls. Granola. Fruit smoothies. The healthy stuff.

Still, nothing changed.

One afternoon during a coaching session, she said what so many new mothers whisper:

> *"I don't understand. I'm trying. I just can't lose anything. Maybe this is just my new normal."*

It was not. She did not need a new normal. She needed new information.

So I asked her to wear a continuous glucose monitor for two weeks. Not for diabetes. Not for weight loss gimmicks. For visibility. I wanted her to see what her body had been trying to tell her for months.

The results showed up fast. It was not just glucose spikes. It was patterns.

Her healthy morning granola was hitting her like she ate a piece of cake.
Her recovery smoothies were sending her on a roller coaster.
Her mid-afternoon energy crashes were directly tied to the quick carbs she grabbed between meetings.
She was not eating poorly. She was eating blindly.

Once she saw the patterns, everything clicked. She said, "I've been trying to fix a problem I never actually understood."

Tina did not overhaul her diet. She adjusted it with precision. She changed the smoothie base. She rebuilt breakfast around protein. She timed snacks to match her biology, not a Pinterest board. Within two weeks her energy steadied. Within a month she dropped her first five pounds.

The win was not the scale. The win was control.

She had been at it for months. Eating clean by her own assessment. Showing up to workouts consistently. But the scale was not moving and her energy was flat. She was convinced she was failing. She was not failing. She was operating without data. When we pulled her actual numbers—sleep quality, daily movement totals, nutrition intake, recovery markers—the picture changed completely. The problem was not effort. It was visibility. She could not course-correct what she could not see. Once the data was on the table, the path forward was obvious. That is the difference between a frustrated participant and a governed operator. One is guessing. The other is reading the dashboard.

That is the difference between noise and signal. When you stop guessing and start measuring, your body stops feeling like a mystery and starts operating like a system you can lead.

The Machine That Removes the Decision

I love innovation—especially when it solves the pain points that sabotage consistency.

When I need a change from the free-weight room, I incorporate the Tonal machine. Not because I am chasing gadgets. Because I did not want a new workout. I wanted a system that runs itself—program, progression, tracking—while I do the work. And if I am going to recommend equipment to clients, it has to earn ROI and save space, not just look impressive.

That is the real value: Tonal reduces decision fatigue. You show up, you work, and the system handles a significant portion of the guessing. It uses adaptive resistance that adjusts based on performance and programming that updates based on recent training history.

> *Tonal is not a chatbot coach. It is an adaptive training engine. It measures what you do, then uses that data to guide the next decision—so you can keep progressing without reinventing your plan every week.*

That is the innovation standard inside EHOS. If the tool does not change a decision, it is noise. If it changes execution, it is infrastructure.

Section 5—AI and the Health Operating System

The Most Powerful Health Tool Most People Are Not Using

The most significant upgrade available to your health operating system right now costs nothing and is available to you tonight. It is not a wearable. It is not a new protocol or a recovery device. It is access to something that used to require a specialist appointment, a waiting list, and several hundred dollars an hour.

It is AI. And most people are using it for everything except their health.

That is about to change. Because when you bring the same discipline to

AI that you have brought to every other chapter in this book—specific questions, real data, a governed framework—it becomes the most powerful accelerant the EHOS loop has ever had.

When Tasha Changed How We Use It

Tasha is precise about everything—her work, her decisions, and her health. So when her annual physical results came back and she saw markers she did not fully understand, she did not wait for a 15-minute follow-up appointment to ask questions she had not yet formed.

She removed her name and all identifying information from the results—sanitized it completely, so it was just the data—and brought it to an AI.

Not to get a diagnosis. Not to replace her physician. To understand what she was looking at before she walked back into that office.

She asked it to explain every marker in plain language—what each one measured, what her specific numbers meant, and which ones were worth discussing at her next appointment.

What came back was not a diagnosis. It was clarity.

She walked into her follow-up appointment with specific, informed questions. Her physician paused and noted that her questions were unusually precise.

That pause is the point. AI did not replace the physician. It made Tasha a more capable participant in the conversation. That is the shift every CEO needs to make—from passive recipient of health information to active, prepared operator.

How to Actually Use It

Most people approach AI the way they approach a search engine. They type a vague question and get a generic answer. A vague question to a doctor produces generic advice. The same is true here. The CEO move is specificity. The more precisely you describe your situation, your goals, and your constraints, the more precisely AI responds.

If you want to understand your lab results, do not ask 'are my results normal?' Ask: 'Here are my lab results from my annual physical. Please explain each marker in plain language—what it measures, what my specific number means, and whether my result is in a healthy range. Then identify the two or three results most worth discussing with my physician and write the specific questions I should ask at my next appointment.' Remove your name and identifying information first. Bring the questions AI generates to your physician—not the AI's interpretation.

If you want a nutrition plan built for your actual life, do not ask for 'healthy meal ideas.' Ask: 'I follow the Single Ingredient Standard—I eat only whole, single-ingredient foods as my baseline. I travel three days a week and work in a corporate environment. Build me a seven-day SIS meal plan with breakfast options I can make in under ten minutes or find in any hotel, three repeatable SIS lunches for a corporate setting, and four SIS dinners I can rotate. My goals are stable energy and maintaining my current weight. Include fifteen staple items I should always have at home to run this plan without thinking.' That prompt produces a working nutrition operating system—not inspiration, execution.

If you want a training program designed for your life, do not ask for 'a good workout routine.' Ask: 'I am a 47-year-old executive with 45 minutes, four days a week to train. My goal is functional strength, joint protection, and cardiovascular health for longevity. I have access to a full gym. Build me a four-day training split with specific exercises, sets, reps, and rest periods. Include one zone 2 cardio session and explain why each element serves my stated goals.' Adjust the age, time, and equipment to match your real life. The structure of the prompt stays the same.

AI as Your Health Education System

This is the application most people never consider and the one that delivers the most lasting value. Most people do not understand the metrics their own body produces. They see VO2 max on their wearable and do not know what to do with it. They hear their physician mention HRV and nod along without understanding what is being measured or why it matters. They receive a fasting glucose number and cannot tell whether to be concerned.

That gap is not a failure of intelligence. It is a failure of access. The medical system was not designed to educate you in 15-minute appointments. AI was.

Ask it to explain VO2 max in plain language—what it measures, what a good number looks like for your age, and what three methods have the strongest evidence for improving it. Ask it to explain what HRV actually tracks, what factors lower it, and what you can do in daily life to protect it. If your physician mentions prediabetes, ask AI what the research shows about reversing it through lifestyle change—specifically, which nutrition, exercise, and sleep habits have the strongest clinical evidence. Do not accept a generic answer. Push for the specific interventions.

This is upskilling applied to your health. You are not looking for shortcuts. You are building the literacy that turns you from a passive recipient of medical information into a governed operator who can participate fully in decisions about your own body. That skill does not expire. It compounds every time you use it.

The Prompt Is the Skill

Here is the insight most executives miss. Using AI is not the skill. Anyone can open a browser and type a question. The skill is knowing how to ask—precisely enough to produce a useful answer, critically enough to evaluate what comes back, and governed enough to know when AI is the right tool and when human judgment is irreplaceable.

That skill—practiced on your health—transfers directly into how you lead your organization. The executive who brings sanitized lab results to an AI and extracts clinical questions from them is practicing the same intellectual discipline as the executive who uses AI to analyze market data, identify operational patterns, or pressure-test a business proposal. The domain is different. The capability is the same.

Your health is not just the enterprise that runs your life. It is the training ground for the most important professional skill of the next decade. Every time you ask a precise health question and evaluate the answer with discipline, you are adding a capability to the resume you are building through this book—one that belongs in every room you walk into.

Vetting Supplements Before You Buy Them

The supplement industry generates over $50 billion annually in the United States. Almost none of it requires FDA pre-approval before it reaches the shelf.

That is not a conspiracy. It is the law. Under DSHEA—the Dietary Supplement Health and Education Act of 1994—supplement manufacturers do not need to prove a product is safe or effective before selling it. The burden falls on the FDA to prove harm after the fact. By the time a product is pulled, millions of people have already purchased it.

Dr. Oz learned this the hard way—publicly. His endorsements of supplements like green coffee bean extract and garcinia cambogia generated enormous sales. When he was called before the U.S. Senate in 2014, senators challenged him directly: where was the evidence? His answer—that he believed in them—was not a clinical defense. It was a marketing position dressed as medical opinion.

The lesson is not about Oz. It is about what happens when credentialed voices are amplified by platforms and compensated by outcomes. The incentive to sell is not the same as the incentive to inform.

Your AI can close this gap. Before you purchase any supplement, run this prompt:

"I am considering taking [supplement name] for [specific goal]. Please summarize what peer-reviewed research actually shows about its effectiveness and safety—not marketing claims or anecdotal evidence. Flag any known risks, drug interactions, or populations for whom it is contraindicated. Tell me the quality of the evidence—is it one small study or multiple large randomized controlled trials? And tell me whether there is an evidence-based alternative I should consider instead."

That prompt does not replace your physician. It walks you into the conversation with the right questions instead of a receipt you cannot return.

One Rule That Governs All of It

AI gives you information. Your physician makes medical decisions.

Those two roles do not compete. They compound each other—but only when you keep them separate. The moment you use AI to avoid your physician, you have crossed from innovation into a liability. The moment you use AI to become a more prepared participant in every health conversation, you have crossed into governance.

Use it like a CEO uses a chief of staff. Not to replace the people who hold expertise and accountability—to ensure you walk into every conversation equipped to lead it.

In EHOS terms, AI does not add a new phase to the loop. It accelerates every phase that already exists. It makes the Assess step sharper because you can interpret your data more completely. It makes the Review step deeper because you can spot patterns across months that daily tracking alone would miss. It makes the Adjust step more precise because you can build plans designed for your actual life, not a generic template. And it makes the Repeat step more consistent because you have a tireless resource available any time the system needs a check-in.

The loop does not change. It runs better.

Kaizen, Not Chaos

A lot of people think improvement requires a dramatic overhaul. Toyota proved the opposite.[6]

The power of the Toyota Production System was not a single breakthrough. It was Kaizen—a culture where small problems get surfaced early and small fixes happen constantly. Not because the company loved meetings. Because tiny leaks become expensive failures if you ignore them long enough.

EHOS works the same way.

Most health breakdowns are not surprise attacks. They are slow leaks: sleep slipping, stress rising, meals getting random, training getting skipped, and your new normal quietly shifting in the wrong direction. Kaizen is how you stop the drift before it becomes damage.

Innovation inside EHOS does not mean reinventing your life. It means running small upgrades that compound:

- One method upgrade per quarter—not twelve new routines.
- One nutrition simplification that reduces decision fatigue.

- One recovery ritual that protects sleep.
- One measurement that reveals a truth you can act on.

If your upgrade adds complexity, it is not an upgrade. It is a leak.

Adrian's Personal Innovation Stack

Tasha's editorial note to me while writing this chapter was direct: tell them what you actually do. Not what sounds impressive. What you actually run.

So here it is. Four things I do that qualify as genuine innovation inside EHOS—not because they are cutting-edge, but because each one changed a decision or removed a friction point that was quietly taxing my system.

The Original Wearable

Before I walk you through my personal stack, there is one concept I want to name because it changes how you think about all of it.

The health and wellness industry has trained people to believe that data comes from devices. You buy the wearable, the wearable collects the data, and now you know something about your body you did not know before.

That is backwards.

Your body has been collecting data since the day you were born. Energy fluctuations. Sleep quality. Hunger patterns. Mood shifts. Recovery speed. Inflammation signals. Cognitive clarity. Your body has been sending all of it, every day, for your entire life. Most people just were not listening.

A wearable does not give you data you never had. It gives you a timestamp and a dashboard for data your body was already generating.

> *You have been collecting data for decades. The device just gives it a timestamp.*

The CEO move is to use devices to confirm what your body is already reporting—not to replace the conversation. My wearables catch what I would otherwise rationalize away—consistency gaps, movement trends, VO2 max trajectory (your aerobic engine capacity—more on this shortly), sessions completed versus planned. The data confirms what my body was already telling me.

Your body is the oldest and most accurate data collection system you own. Devices are confirmation tools, not replacement tools. Learn to read both.

1. Adaptive Training Systems—Eliminating Training Decision Fatigue

When I step in front of the Tonal, the decision-making is already done. What to train, how much weight to use, how to progress—the system handles all of it. My only job is to show up and execute. That is not laziness. That is what a well-governed system looks like when it is running correctly. You do not rebuild the engine every morning. You turn the key and drive.

2. Seasonal Rotation—Treadmill to Outdoor, Winter to Spring

I rotate my cardio base by season. When the weather is unreliable, I use the treadmill—controlled, predictable, no excuses. The moment the weather breaks, I am outside. Three to five miles, walking or running, depending on the day.

Same mission. Different stimulus. This serves two purposes. It keeps execution from getting stale, which protects adherence. And it gives the body a different physical demand—outdoor terrain, variable pace, environmental exposure—without adding complexity. The standard does not change. The method rotates.

3. Controlled Experimentation—The Red Team Approach

In cybersecurity, red teaming is the practice of deliberately attacking your own system before an adversary does. A red team does not guess where the vulnerability is. It builds a structured experiment with a specific objective, a defined timeline, and a measurable outcome—and it runs the test until the system either holds or breaks. Either result is useful. Both produce data.

After over 30 years in corporate cybersecurity, I brought this same logic into my health experiments. Every new training protocol, recovery tool, or nutrition change gets run as a red team test—not a hopeful addition, but a controlled experiment. What is the specific outcome I am measuring? What is the timeline? What threshold tells me this worked or did not? Without those three parameters defined in advance, you are not running an experiment. You are running a feeling.

The practical version: pick one variable—a training stimulus, a sleep protocol, a recovery tool—and run it as a 30-day red team. Define what success looks like before you start. Track the single metric that matters most. At the end of 30 days, make a binary decision: integrate or discard. This prevents two expensive errors simultaneously— abandoning something that needed more time and keeping something that stopped delivering.

4. VO2 Max Tracking—A Leading Indicator of Long-Term Health and Performance

VO2 max is the maximum amount of oxygen your body can use during sustained exercise. In plain terms: it measures your aerobic engine. And your aerobic engine strongly correlates with how well you recover, perform, and age.

I track mine through wearables. Not because I need laboratory precision, but because the trend line tells the truth. A rising VO2 max means the engine is getting stronger. A declining one is an early warning that something upstream—sleep, stress, training consistency— is breaking down.

In EHOS terms, VO2 max is the health equivalent of cash flow. You do not need perfect numbers. You need the trend moving in the right direction.

Method	What It Measures	CEO Application
Zone 2 Training (Long-Term ROI Builder)	Steady conversational cardio. You can talk but not sing. Builds aerobic engine and mitochondrial efficiency.	30–45 min brisk walk, incline treadmill, cycling, or rowing. Highest ROI for the time invested. The compounding interest of fitness.
High-Intensity Intervals (Quick Accelerator)	Short bursts of high effort followed by recovery. Spikes heart rate, challenges the system, lifts VO2 max fast.	60 sec fast, 2 min slow. Repeat 6–10 times. Add one session per week to an existing training plan.
Strength Training (Power Multiplier)	Muscles use oxygen. More muscle = more demand = better aerobic efficiency and a stronger engine.	Compound movements: squats, deadlifts, rows, presses. Protects capacity as you age. The structural foundation of EHOS.

The three methods above are not complicated. They are well-established. And they compound: zone 2 training builds the engine, intervals accelerate it, and strength training gives it structural support. Add one. Run it for a quarter. Measure the trend.

SECTION 8 — R&D SPRINT: ROTATE BY SEASON, UPGRADE ONLY IF ROI IS REAL

Run Controlled Experiments. Not Random Change.

Your body adapts. Your mind gets bored. Your schedule shifts. So you rotate on purpose.

Treat method rotation the way a good executive treats R&D: controlled, time-boxed, and judged by evidence.

- Test one variable—not five.
- Run it long enough to tell the truth.
- Keep the primary KPI constant: commitments kept.
- Kill it fast if adherence drops.

And here is the noise filter, because the internet is a landfill of fake innovation: if someone is claiming unreal results on social media with a product you have never heard of, treat it with the same skepticism you would apply to a pitch deck from someone with no revenue. EHOS does not run on miracles. It runs on systems.

1. Identify one health tool, app, or device you currently use or are considering. Run it through the three-question innovation filter before the week ends: Does it change a decision? Does it remove friction? Does it reveal a signal you can act on? If it fails all three, it is clutter. Cut it or redesign how you use it.
2. Pick one health topic you do not fully understand—VO2 max, HRV, a lab result, a condition your physician mentioned. Bring a specific question to an AI tonight. Practice the prompt discipline: specific situation, real constraints, clear goal. Then bring what you learn to your next physician or board conversation.
3. Design one Background Update for next quarter. One small upgrade to your existing system—one nutrition adjustment, one recovery addition, one measurement you will start tracking. One change. Write it down before closing this chapter.

EXECUTIVE DEBRIEF

Innovation is not novelty—it is infrastructure that improves execution. The F1 mindset reframed the standard: change the right variable, not all of them. The Background Update turned improvement from emergency maintenance into a quiet, compounding discipline. AI put a brilliant health advisor in your pocket. And the controlled experiment framework stopped the two most expensive errors simultaneously—quitting too early and keeping what stopped working.

"If the upgrade does not change a decision, it is noise.
If it changes execution, it is infrastructure."

Complete this Operating Sheet in the book, or log your answers directly into the EHOS Dashboard at adrianmwilliams.com. Members with a free account can access all worksheets, save their responses by chapter, and generate their CEO of Me Health Resume automatically from their answers.

Executive Action 1—One Tool to Evaluate: Run the innovation filter on one tool you currently use or are considering. Does it change a decision? Remove friction? Reveal a signal? Tool: _______________ Decision: Keep / Cut / Redesign

Figure 7.3 *KPI Tier System — Tracking Framework (Reference)*

KPI Tier	What to Track	Options
Primary KPI (pick 1 — your scoreboard)	The one number you cannot negotiate with. Tracks weekly. Consistent progress = commitments kept.	Training sessions completed Sleep window protected (nights/week) SIS baseline meals (per week) Movement minutes or steps (weekly)
Supporting KPIs (pick 2–4 — the drivers)	The inputs that explain why your primary KPI moves. Track weekly.	Protein-first breakfast (days/week) Afternoon crash avoided (days/week) Strength sessions (days/week) Bedtime window hit (days/week) Water target hit (days/week)
Risk KPI (pick 1 — early warning)	The lagging indicator that predicts future cost. Review monthly or quarterly.	Weight trend (weekly average) Waistline trend (monthly) Blood pressure trend (monthly) Annual physical + labs
Signal vs. Noise Rules	If it does not change a decision, it is noise. If tracking becomes the job, you will quit the job. One scoreboard. Small driver set. Execute.	

Figure 7.4 *My KPI Stack — Personal Selection Template*

My KPI Stack	Selection
Primary KPI (my scoreboard this season)	_______________________________
Supporting KPIs (pick 2–4)	1. _______________________________ 2. _______________________________ 3. _______________________________
Risk KPI (early warning — review monthly)	_______________________________
Review cadence	Daily awareness (light touch) Weekly Executive Review (10 minutes) Monthly deeper check Quarterly portfolio audit

Executive Action 2—One Health Topic to Research with AI: Pick one metric or condition you want to understand better. Write your specific prompt before closing this chapter. Topic: _______________________________ My prompt: _______________________________

Executive Action 3—One Background Update for Next Quarter: One small upgrade to your existing system. The variable: _______________________ The timeline: _______________________ What success looks like: _______________________

Figure 7.5 *EHOS Innovation Filter — Signal vs. Noise Decision Framework*

Filter / Rule	Question to Answer
Decision test	What decision will this tool or method improve? (sleep, training, food, recovery, or risk)
Friction test	What friction will this remove? (planning, tracking, guessing, or inconsistency)
Signal test	What truth will it reveal that I can act on? If you cannot answer this in one sentence, do not buy it.

Adoption standard	If you will not use it weekly, do not buy it. If it adds complexity, it is a leak. If it reduces decision fatigue and improves adherence, it is infrastructure.
R&D Sprint rule	Test one variable, not five. Run it long enough to tell the truth. Keep the primary KPI constant (commitments kept). Kill it fast if adherence drops.
Noise filter	If it only works when conditions are perfect, it is not a system. If someone is claiming unreal results on social media, it is probably not real. EHOS runs on systems, not miracles.

Audio book listeners and website visitors: download this table at adrianmwilliams.com

Figure 7.6 *30-Day Health R&D Sprint — Controlled Experimentation Template*

Sprint Element	Your Answer
Variable I am testing (one change only)	______________________
What stays constant (primary KPI)	______________________
Sprint duration (4–8 weeks recommended)	______________________
Success criteria (one sentence)	______________________
Decision at sprint end	Keep it / Modify it / Kill it Reason: ______________________

Audio book listeners and website visitors: download this table at adrianmwilliams.com

Congratulations—You've Earned These Skills

Health Resilience Operator—Deployed real-time operational tools—obstacle removal, strategic variety, and environment governance—to sustain health execution through disrupted weeks without restarting the system from zero.

Obstacle Removal Specialist—Applied a structured friction-identification and removal protocol to convert execution breakdowns from personal failures into solvable engineering problems, maintaining system continuity under real-world pressure.

HEALTH ENVIRONMENT ARCHITECT—AUDITED AND RESTRUCTURED DEFAULT ENVIRONMENTAL SETTINGS AND SOCIAL OCCASION PROTOCOLS TO REDUCE FRICTION AND REINFORCE MISSION-ALIGNED DEFAULTS.

Chapter Eight

Personal Branding and Rebranding

Your Health Is Not What You Claim. It Is What Your Habits Prove.

Your brand is not your announcement. It is your operating behavior—especially when nobody is watching.

The system is upgraded. Chapter 8 asks the harder question: does the person running it match the standard it is producing?

Innovation means nothing if the brand it serves is not aligned.

Branding is not something that happens to companies. It happens to people. Every day. Through every choice. The question is not whether you have a health brand. You already do. The question is whether it is the one you intended.

The Rock's Strategic Reinvention—And Why He Had To

Dwayne Johnson did not just rebuild his brand once.[1] He has rebuilt it several times with the precision of a CEO who understands that longevity requires evolution, not just endurance.

For years, Johnson was known for the relentless grind. Before-sunrise workouts. Herculean meals. A body built on intensity and iron discipline. But as he entered his fifties, the same formula that made him a global powerhouse began working against him. His joints carried decades of punishment from wrestling. Recovery lagged behind ambition. Stress mounted under nonstop productivity.

He hit a point many leaders eventually face: the operating model that built success could no longer sustain it.

Instead of hiding the shift, Johnson did something rare in performance culture. He told the truth. He acknowledged the toll. He talked about mental health. He dropped the facade of invincibility. And with that honesty came a rebrand far more powerful than any promotional tour.

He pivoted toward longevity. He restructured training around mobility and joint preservation. He overhauled nutrition with a focus on inflammation control. He integrated recovery, therapy, and self-awareness into his identity. He started showing the world that health is not about lifting the heaviest weight—it is about carrying the right weight. Physically, mentally, emotionally.

> *If your habits do not evolve with your life, they*
> *eventually break you.*

Johnson's evolution sent a message that every executive needs to hear: rebranding is not cosmetic. It is operational. The routines, beliefs, and standards that built your success five years ago may not be able to carry your future. Reinvention is not weakness. It is wisdom applied to the next version of the system.

> *A brand built on performance collapses when the audience leaves. A*
> *brand built on execution holds regardless of who is watching.*

Whether You Realize It or Not, You Are Branding Yourself Every Day

Your actions, choices, and habits communicate something about who you are—loudly and clearly. Your diet. Your energy. Your discipline. Your consistency. All of it tells a story.

To those around you, your energy, your presence, and the way you carry yourself communicate something—whether you intend the message or not. How you show up physically tells a story before you say a word.

On the other hand, if you are making healthy choices—consistent, intentional, disciplined—that becomes your brand. People notice. People respect it. And over time, it becomes the expectation others hold of you—and the standard you hold of yourself.

The Bet That Built My Brand

There was a time when drinking was part of my brand. It was normal. Expected. Then I made a bet with my wife. She would stop shopping for six months, and I would stop drinking for six months. I am competitive, so I had to do it.

We both made the six months. She went back to shopping. I never went back to drinking.

I hit a point where I knew I could not say I stood for health while still living in contradiction. So I made the call to stop. I have kept that standard since 2016.

Now people know I do not drink. That is part of my identity. If there is a dinner or social gathering, they already know not to offer me alcohol. I do not eat at buffets—not because I am trying to be difficult, but because it does not align with how I treat my body. At family functions, if there are no healthy options, I simply do not eat. I usually eat beforehand or find something aligned with my goals when I get home.

Even at formal banquets, if the menu does not support my wellness, I do not make exceptions. Consistency is part of my brand. Discipline is part of my brand. What I say matches what I do. That is powerful.

My brand is also teaching. I want to help others move beyond momentary health fixes and embrace sustainable, long-term wellness. I do not promote trends—I promote longevity. Everything I do is evaluated through one lens: can I still be doing this at 80 or 90 years old?

> *A real brand is not your intention. It is your standard—the behavior you refuse to negotiate.*

You Cannot Permanently Change Your Habits Until You Change Who You Believe You Are

Most people think change begins with habits. They try to eat cleaner, wake up earlier, or train more consistently. But here is the truth: you cannot permanently change your habits until you change who you believe you are.

Habits are operational—they run on systems. Identity is strategic—it defines the system.

A new habit built on an old identity is like installing new software on a corrupted operating system. It may work for a while. But eventually, the bugs show up.

Reframe the narrative: "I am a person who eats intentionally." That one shift turns effort into evidence. You are no longer trying to become healthy. You are proving who you already are.

The strongest product launches happen when identity and product are already aligned. The same principle applies to you—when who you believe you are matches the habits you are trying to build, execution stops feeling like resistance.

Your goal is not to add more habits. It is to become someone who naturally lives by better ones. When identity and actions are aligned, willpower becomes irrelevant. You stop fighting to do what is right and start defaulting to it.

Before you redesign your diet, your training, or your sleep schedule, start with the blueprint of you. Ask yourself:

- What kind of person achieves the outcomes I want?
- How would that version of me think, act, and make decisions daily?
- What systems would they protect? What standards would they never negotiate?

That is the pivot point—from trying to change behavior to transforming belief. Once the identity shifts, the habits follow.

In EHOS terms, identity is not a separate step—it is what makes the Repeat phase hold. A system run by someone who believes they are the kind of person who executes runs differently than one run by someone trying to become that person.

Under Armour Did Not Grow by Accident—and Neither Will Your Brand

When Kevin Plank founded Under Armour, he established a clear brand mission: providing high-performance gear to empower athletes.[2] That explicit definition guided every business decision—design, marketing, partnerships, and product lines. Clarity of identity made every choice easier because the filter was already set.

Your health brand needs the same clarity. Without it, every decision becomes a negotiation.

My health brand stands for three things: disciplined, intentional, and consistent. It reflects alignment between what I value and how I show up. I review it quarterly to make sure it still matches who I am becoming— not just who I have been.

Here is the Brand Gap Scan. Run it now. Under two minutes.

Figure 8.1 *Brand Gap Scan — Standards Audit*

Brand Gap Scan	Your Answer
What do I do consistently— no matter what? (That is your real brand.)	
What do I allow to slide first? (That is your risk exposure.)	
What is the smallest standard I can enforce this week that proves integrity? (That is your rebrand starting point.)	

If your answers do not match the identity you claim—disciplined, energized, built for longevity—your brand is not your words. It is your data.

> *Rebranding is not reinvention. It is realignment—closing the gap between what you say matters and what you actually do.*

External Change Means Nothing Without Internal Transformation

When most people think about rebranding, they think about optics—how they appear to others, how they carry themselves, what image they project. But true health rebranding is not an external makeover. It is an internal alignment.

You can tell the world you are healthy. You can post the gym selfie, order the salad at dinner, and talk about what you used to do. But if your daily habits—when nobody is watching—do not match that identity, your brand is not changing. What you consistently do is what builds your brand.

Most people get exposed here. They try to rebrand with announcements instead of deposits.

George—The Friend Who Finally Stopped Talking

I have a friend named George. For years, George talked nonstop about what he was going to do or what he used to do. 'I used to run, bike, hike—I did it all.' 'I am about to start walking again.' For a long time, that was his brand: nostalgia and potential. Nothing current. Nothing consistent.

But over time, George shifted—not overnight, but gradually. He started walking and working out four to five times a week. He cut back on sugar. No more daily honey buns. He stopped overeating. Those quiet decisions became his real brand. Not the stories. Not the intentions. The execution. He lost more than 90 pounds. And when he gets off track now—because life happens to everyone—he knows exactly what to do to get back on. No drama. No restart speech. Just the next rep.

That is what internal rebranding looks like. It is not a crash diet. It is not a gym membership you use twice. It is the moment you stop negotiating with the standards you say you live by—and you start acting like the person you claim to be.

You already have the infrastructure for this. The Health Portfolio. The strategy. The operating cadence. The only remaining question is whether your private behavior is aligned with the identity you say you are building.

Private Wins are the actions nobody applauds. They are the deposits nobody sees. They are also the only actions that permanently build a brand. Every time you execute when no one is watching, you are not just building a habit—you are building the evidence that you are who you say you are.

Figure 8.2 *Private Win Protocol — Weekly Execution Standard*

Private Win Protocol	Your Execution
Standard I will not negotiate this week:	
How I make it easy to execute and hard to avoid:	
How I prove it quietly—then repeat until it is identity:	

SECTION 6—SIGNS YOU NEED A HEALTH REBRAND

Brands Do Not Collapse Overnight—They Drift First

A business does not wake up one day and suddenly lose market position. The drift happens first. Small compromises. Quiet inconsistencies. A few missed decisions that feel harmless—until the numbers force a reckoning.

Your health works the same way. Here are the five signals that your current brand and your desired brand are no longer aligned:

1. Your non-negotiables became negotiable. If the behaviors you claimed were standards are now "when I have time," your brand already shifted.
2. You are performing health, not executing health. Talking about the plan. Buying the gear. Posting the moment. But the deposits—sleep, movement, meals, recovery—are not consistent.

3. *You keep paying the same Pain Tax in different forms. The same breakdown shows up again: energy crashes, weight rebound, stress eating, missed workouts, sleep drift. New packaging. Same root cause: unmanaged systems.*

4. You cannot trust your own word anymore. If you are constantly renegotiating with yourself, you do not have a motivation problem. You have an integrity problem. Brands break when promises break.

5. Your current routine cannot survive real life. Travel, deadlines, family, stress—if your system collapses under pressure, it is not a system. It is a fair-weather plan.

If two or more of those are true right now, you do not need more motivation. You need a rebrand. Run the Brand Gap Scan from Section 4. Start with one standard this week. Prove it quietly. Then repeat.

> *Drift is not failure. Drift is data. The CEO move is to catch it early and correct before it becomes default.*

A Setback Is a Forced Rebrand. Not a Pause. Not a Pity Party. A Redesign.

Every powerful brand reaches a moment when the story must change. Not because the brand lost its value—but because the engine behind it can no longer run on the same fuel.

A setback does not just pause your progress. It confronts the version of you that was built on momentum, routine, or sheer force of will. It exposes the gap between how you have been operating and what your body actually needs to sustain you.

Kevin Hart is a modern example of a forced rebrand—because his comeback was not motivational. It was operational.

In September 2019, Hart was involved in a serious car accident that fractured his spine in three places.[3] Surgeons told him he was fortunate to be walking. He was told recovery would take years.

Most people in that position try to get back to who they were as fast as possible. Hart did something smarter. He documented the actual work—not the highlight, not the comeback moment, but the daily grind of learning to move again. The physical therapy sessions. The one-pound dumbbell days. The moment of trying to put on a shirt and realizing his body was not cooperating. He showed what a real rebuild looks like: slow, humbling, and completely non-negotiable.

He also told the truth about the mental weight of it. The frustration of going from one of the most physically capable performers in entertainment to someone who needed help with basic movement. That honesty did not damage his brand. It deepened it. Because it proved the brand was never built on performance—it was built on discipline, resilience, and the willingness to do the work nobody applauds.

His return was not a sprint back to the old model. He rebuilt training around what his spine could actually support. He restructured his schedule to protect recovery. He adjusted his identity from machine to operator who knows his system. The brand did not shrink. It evolved.

That is the CEO lesson embedded in Hart's story: a setback is not the end of the brand. It is a full-system audit that forces you to rebuild with better materials—more sustainable, more honest, and better aligned to who you are actually becoming.

The CEO move after a setback is not more motivation. It is governance. You tell the truth about capacity. You redesign the system. You rebuild the brand around what is sustainable—not what is impressive.

My Own Forced Rebrand

Setbacks have humanized my brand. They reminded me to lead with sustainability, not ego. Rebranding after injury meant shifting from beast mode to longevity mode. Recovery became a strategy, not a weakness. I stopped chasing what looked impressive and started protecting what was sustainable.

In practice that meant redesigning training to protect joints and preserve movement quality. Treating recovery—sleep, mobility, stress downshifts— as a core deliverable. Rebuilding consistency with minimum standards instead of maximum intensity.

When your body forces a reset, the worst decision is pretending you are the same operator with the same capacity. That is how reinjury happens. That is how the brand becomes "starts strong, fades fast."

When life shrinks your bandwidth—injury, illness, a season of genuine overload—the CEO move is not to pretend your capacity is unchanged. You update your identity to match reality without abandoning the mission. You do not sprint back to who you were. You architect the next version of who you are becoming.

Figure 8.3 *Constraint Rebrand — Setback Recovery Protocol*

Constraint Rebrand Element	Your Answer
What triggered the setback? (injury, illness, life disruption)	
Honest capacity right now: What can I do this week without paying the Pain Tax later?	
Anchor behavior I will protect (one: sleep, movement, or nutrition)	
Minimum standard this season (one sentence)	
Identity statement I am operating from:	I am someone who ___________
When I return to full capacity, the first standard I restore is:	

Setbacks do not destroy brands. Denial does.

Accountability Without Performance

If your health communication is performance, you will quit when the applause fades. If it is accountability, you will keep going when nobody claps.

There is another version that is accountability—sharing with the specific purpose of creating a structure that supports follow-through. When nobody claps, you keep going anyway because the system does not run on attention.

Social media—Instagram, TikTok, LinkedIn—can support accountability when used intentionally. But it is not necessary to broadcast everything. You can share with a close group of friends, a private community, or one trusted person and get the same benefit: support, structure, and accountability without the performance pressure.

I use social media selectively. It is less about flexing and more about documenting process. Community can amplify commitment—but only when the sharing serves execution, not the other way around.

Your goal is not attention. Your goal is integrity. Share enough to create accountability and support—not so much that the sharing becomes the work.

Your Health Board is your most important accountability structure. Social media is optional. The board is not. If you have built your board correctly, you already have the accountability you need—and sharing publicly becomes a choice, not a requirement.

Figure 8.4 *Selective Accountability — Channel and Governance Template*

Selective Accountability Element	Your Decision
Channel (one person, small private group, or private tracking):	
Cadence (weekly is enough — consistency beats volume):	
Report format (one win, one risk, one next move):	

1. Run the Brand Gap Scan from Section 4 today. Three questions. Under two minutes. Write the answers on Operating Sheet 8 without editing or softening them. Whatever shows up is your current brand—not your intended brand, your actual one. The gap between those two answers is your rebrand starting point.

2. Define your health brand in three words on Operating Sheet 8. Then list three non-negotiable behaviors that prove those words. If you cannot list three, you have one job this week: identify the first one and execute it without negotiation. That is how a brand becomes real—one deposit at a time.

3. If you are recovering from a setback—injury, illness, or a season that shrunk your capacity—complete the Setback Recovery section of Operating Sheet 8. Tell the truth about current capacity, name your one anchor behavior, and write your identity statement for this season.

EXECUTIVE DEBRIEF

What you do consistently—especially when no one is watching—is your brand. Not your intentions. Not your announcements. Not the gear you buy or the posts you share. The deposits. The private wins. The standards you refuse to negotiate when it would be easier not to. That is what builds something that lasts.

"Your health brand is not what you claim.
It is what your habits prove when nobody is watching."

OPERATING SHEET 8—YOUR HEALTH BRAND

Complete this Operating Sheet in the book, or log your answers directly into the EHOS Dashboard at adrianmwilliams.com. Members with a free account can access all worksheets, save their responses by chapter, and generate their CEO of Me Health Resume automatically from their answers.

Executive Action 1—Brand Gap Scan: What do I do consistently no matter what? What do I allow to slide first? What is the smallest standard I can enforce this week to prove integrity?

**Executive Action 2—My Health Brand in Three Words + Three Non-Negotiables: My brand stands for: _______ ______ ______.
Non-negotiable 1: ___ Non-negotiable 2: ___ Non-negotiable 3: ___**

Health Brand Definition

Purpose: Define your health brand in plain language and connect it to behaviors you can execute and measure.

Executive Action 3—Setback Recovery (complete only if applicable): What triggered the setback: ___ Honest capacity right now: ___ My one anchor behavior this season: ___ My identity statement: 'I am someone who _________'

Constraint Rebrand—Setback Recovery Protocol

Purpose: Rebuild health execution and identity after injury, illness, or life disruption without losing mission alignment.

Congratulations—You've Earned These Skills

Brand Dimension	Honest Answer	Gap?
What do I do consistently—no matter what? (This is your real brand.)		Yes / No
What do I allow to slide first? (This is your risk exposure.)		Yes / No
What do I say about my health in public?		Yes / No
What do I actually do when nobody is watching?		Yes / No
Do my private habits match my stated identity?		Yes / No
Smallest standard I can enforce this week to prove integrity:		—

Health Brand Architect—Defined a personal health brand grounded in non-negotiable behavioral standards, closing the gap between stated identity and daily execution across all life conditions.

HEALTH IDENTITY STRATEGIST—ESTABLISHED A CLEAR PERSONAL HEALTH IDENTITY THAT DRIVES EXECUTION FROM THE INSIDE OUT, SO HEALTHY BEHAVIOR BECOMES WHO YOU ARE RATHER THAN WHAT YOU FORCE YOURSELF TO DO.

Setback Rebranding Specialist—Applied the Constraint Rebrand protocol to redesign health execution after disruption, maintaining mission alignment without requiring full-capacity performance.

The brand is defined. Chapter 9 protects it for life—not for a season, not until the next goal, but for the long arc. Because the most important question is not who you are today. It is whether the system you have built is designed to keep you that way.

Element	Your Answer
My health brand stands for (3 words maximum):	_______ _______ _______
Non-negotiable #1 (behavior I never compromise):	_______________
Non-negotiable #2:	_______________
Non-negotiable #3:	_______________
Brand-breaking habit I am eliminating this quarter:	_______________
Brand-building habit I am installing this quarter:	_______________
How I want to be known in 12 months:	_______________

Constraint Rebrand Element	Your Answer
What triggered the setback? (injury, illness, life disruption)	
Honest capacity right now: What can I do this week without paying the Pain Tax later?	
Anchor behavior I will protect (one: sleep, movement, or nutrition)	
Minimum standard this season (one sentence)	
Identity statement I am operating from:	I am someone who __________
When I return to full capacity, the first standard I restore is:	

Sustainable Health Practices
The Retention Problem Nobody Is Solving.

Most people do not fail at health because they lack commitment. They fail because they built a plan that was never designed to last.

Chapter 9 is not more instruction. It is the diagnosis. The answer to the one question nobody in the health industry wants to ask out loud: Why do plans that start strong always seem to end the same way? And what does a plan that is designed from the start—architecturally, deliberately, without assuming a good week—actually look like?

This is the chapter most health books get wrong. They treat sustainability as a motivational problem. More inspiration. More accountability partners. More reminders of your "why."

It is not a motivational problem. It is a systems design problem. And it has a solution.

Amazon Prime Did Not Build a Product. It Built a Retention System.

When Amazon launched Prime in 2005, the pitch was simple: pay an annual fee, get free two-day shipping. On the surface, it looked like a logistics offer. Underneath, it was one of the most sophisticated retention systems ever engineered.

Jeff Bezos was not trying to acquire more customers. He was trying to make leaving more costly than staying.

The moment someone paid for Prime membership, their behavior changed. They browsed more. They bought more. They started to feel that not using Prime was wasting money they had already spent. Amazon then systematically added value—video streaming, music, photo storage, early access to deals—not to make the product flashier, but to deepen the switching cost. Every new feature made the question "why would I leave?" harder to answer.

Amazon did not just create switching costs. They built something so woven into daily behavior—so convenient, so frictionless, so much a part of how people lived and shopped—that leaving felt like losing something, not just canceling a subscription. That is the difference between a product people use and a system people live inside.

Amazon never asked "how do we get people excited about us?" They asked: "why do people leave, and how do we make staying the path of least resistance?" Every decision—pricing, feature sequencing, default behaviors—was built around that single question.

> *Most people treat health like a product launch. CEOs treat it like a retention problem.*

Your health operates on exactly the same economics. Starting is cheap. Staying is the hard part. The gap between the two is not willpower. It is systems design.

Domino's CEO Patrick Doyle did something rare: instead of defending the product or redirecting with marketing spend, he acknowledged the feedback publicly and rebuilt from scratch. Whether driven by conviction or necessity, the decision proved that fixing the actual problem outperforms promoting around it every time.

Domino's ran national ads showing real customer complaints. They reformulated the dough, the sauce, the cheese. They rebuilt the delivery experience. And they tracked every metric with obsessive precision—not to prove the rebrand was working to shareholders, but to catch problems before they became defaults.

The result was one of the most sustained corporate turnarounds in restaurant history—measurable, compounding, and driven entirely by system change rather than marketing. Not because they ran a great campaign. Because they fixed the system that was causing people to leave—and then built the feedback loops to make sure it never broke the same way again.

Two companies. Two industries. One principle: the organizations that win long-term are not the ones that launch the best. They are the ones that build systems specifically designed to prevent the exit.

Your health is no different. Most plans are designed like a product launch—generate excitement, drive early results, create momentum. Almost none of them are designed like Amazon Prime—engineered from day one to make staying the default and leaving the exception.

That is the architecture this chapter builds.

> *Discipline alone is not a strategy. It is raw potential. Without a retention system behind it, it collapses the moment real life applies pressure.*

Intensity Without Sustainability Is Just an Expensive Starting Point

You may have seen it. The Biggest Loser ran from 2004 to 2016 and at its peak drew millions of viewers every week. The premise was simple: take severely overweight contestants, put them in a controlled environment with elite trainers and nutritionists, and film the transformation. Dramatic weight loss. Emotional breakthroughs. A cash prize for whoever lost the most. What the show never answered—and what the follow-up research exposed—was what happened after the cameras stopped.

Follow-up research told the real story: significant weight regain and persistent metabolic adaptation that lasted years after the competition ended.[1] The problem was not willpower. The problem was a strategy engineered for a controlled environment that does not exist in real life.

Most people do exactly the same thing on a smaller scale. They start at maximum intensity—six workouts a week, complete diet overhaul, early mornings, zero exceptions. It works for two weeks. Then real life shows up. Then the intensity becomes unsustainable. Then they quit. Then they blame themselves.

Research shows that approximately 80 percent of people who start a new fitness routine abandon it within five months—not because they stop caring, but because the plan was never designed to survive real life.[2] The Biggest Loser contestants are the most public example. But it plays out in every gym, every January, every time a plan was built for maximum intensity instead of maximum durability.

I call this the Sprint Trap—what happens when you design a health plan for your best-case schedule and then try to execute it through your real one. The plan was never the problem. The design was.

The fix is not less ambition. It is smarter architecture. Start at 60 percent of what you think you can sustain. Run that for 30 days. Then scale. The goal in month one is not transformation. The goal in month one is proof of concept—evidence that this plan can survive contact with your actual life.

Think of it like the drip bucket versus the bathtub. A bucket placed under a slow leak will fill—it takes longer, but it fills completely, without losing a drop. Turn on the bathtub faucet at full blast and water splashes everywhere. It looks like more is happening. Less actually lands.

Health transformation is more like watching grass grow than watching fireworks. You do not notice it every single day. But one morning you look up and the landscape has completely changed. That is how lasting progress works—quiet, steady, and compounding.

Real health transformation is not about going hard. It is about going long.

If your health plan only works in a controlled bubble, it is not a strategy. It is a temporary campaign. A real strategy survives volatility—travel, deadlines, illness, grief, transition, and the ordinary chaos of a full life.

The Sustainable Operating Model has three components. Together they answer the three questions every health plan must answer to survive real life.

Figure 9.1 *Sustainable Operating Model (SOM) — Three-Element Framework*

SOM Element	Definition	Your Version
Minimum Standard (MS) The floor, not the goal	The smallest version of your plan you will execute on your worst week. Non-negotiable. Not optional.	______________ ______________
Operating Rhythm (OR) The default, not the decision	The repeatable daily and weekly cadence that removes decision fatigue. The system runs. You execute.	______________ ______________
Relapse Trigger Reset (RTR) The threshold, not the rule	Your pre-decided Danger Zone threshold for each domain. When crossed: stabilize, simplify, return to fundamentals. No emotion. No new plan.	______________ ______________

Most plans are designed with a Minimum Standard and an Operating Rhythm—and then left open at the third element. When disruption arrives, there is no pre-decided response. So the person improvises. And improvisation under stress almost always regresses toward the old default.

The Relapse Trigger Reset closes that gap. It is not a list of rules. It is a pre-decided threshold—specific, measurable, and tied directly to the Danger Zone framework in Section 4. When a threshold is crossed, the reset is automatic: stabilize, simplify, return to fundamentals. No deliberation. No new plan. No waiting for motivation to show up.

The difference between a Minimum Standard and a Relapse Trigger Reset is the direction they face. The Minimum Standard faces forward—it tells you the least you will do on a good day. The Relapse Trigger Reset faces inward—it tells you exactly what happens the moment the system breaks down. Both are required. Neither works without the other.

Complete your operating model on Operating Sheet 9 before this week ends. One sentence per element. If you cannot write your Minimum Standard in one sentence, it is too complex to execute under pressure. If you cannot name your Relapse Trigger Reset threshold, you do not yet have a plan—you have an intention.

Why People Quit—and the System That Stops Each One

Most people think they quit because they lack discipline. They do not. They quit because their plan had no system to catch the four specific moments where health execution breaks down. Every one of them is predictable. Every one of them is preventable.

Failure Mode	What It Looks Like	The Fix
The Sprint Trap	Start at maximum intensity. Burn out in weeks. Quit. Blame willpower.	Start at 60% of what you think you can do. Scale up after 30 days of consistent execution.
The Danger Zone (no threshold set)	Drift is invisible. Small compromises stack. Default quietly shifts in the wrong direction.	Pre-define your Danger Zone thresholds in advance. When triggered: stabilize,
The 24-Hour Rule	Miss one day. Tell yourself a story. Miss the next day. Now it is a habit.	Never miss twice. One miss is an event. Two misses is a pattern. Three misses is a new default.
The Victory Debt	Hit a milestone. Brain declares victory. Standards soften. Tracking disappears. Drift returns.	After every win, immediately set the next micro-target. Victory is a checkpoint, not a finish line.

Failure Mode 1—The Sprint Trap (covered in Section 2)

Design for your worst week, not your best. If the plan requires ideal conditions to survive, the plan is not ready.

Failure Mode 2—The Danger Zone

In business, strong leaders do not wait for a crisis to confirm something is wrong. They define guardrails in advance. Revenue drops past a certain threshold, costs rise beyond tolerance, customer churn spikes—and action is immediate, not eventual.

Health deserves the same discipline. The Danger Zone is your personal set of pre-decided, non-negotiable thresholds. The line you have already committed to not crossing.

This matters because health breakdowns almost never happen suddenly. They happen quietly. A few skipped workouts. Slightly looser food choices. Small compromises that feel harmless in isolation but compound over time into a new default.

Here is what the Danger Zone looks like in real life. If your healthy operating weight is 185 pounds and the scale reads 195 for five consecutive days, that is not a bad week. That is operational drift. At that point, decisive action is not punishment. It is leadership.

Decisive does not mean extreme. It means you go back to your core principles—the ones you defined when things were working—without negotiation, without drama, without waiting to feel motivated.

The same applies to sleep, nutrition, training, and daily movement. Pre-define the threshold for each one. Write it down on Operating Sheet 9. Because when you are in the Danger Zone, you will not think clearly. You need a decision you already made.

When the Danger Zone is triggered, your job is not to be perfect. Your job is to stabilize, simplify, and execute the fundamentals until momentum returns. Not quitting is the objective. Consistency is the strategy. The Danger Zone is the safeguard.

Failure Mode 3—The 24-Hour Rule

Missing a day is not the problem. What you tell yourself about missing a day is the problem.

Here is the sequence that destroys most health plans. You miss a workout. Instead of treating it as a neutral event—one missed execution in a long operating history—you attach a story to it. "I always do this." "I have no discipline." "I knew I couldn't stick to it." That story makes missing the next day feel inevitable. Now you have missed twice. Three times. The story becomes a belief. The belief becomes a new default.

I call this the 24-Hour Rule: never miss twice. One miss is an event. Two misses is a pattern. Three misses is a new default. The rule is not about perfection—it is about identity protection.

The 24-Hour Rule removes the story entirely. You missed. The next execution window is within 24 hours. That is the only decision on the table. No spiral. No assessment of your character. No fresh start speech. Just the next rep.

One miss followed by one return is a person with discipline. One miss followed by a story is a person building a reason to quit. You control which one you are—not by motivation, but by the rule you follow after a miss.

Failure Mode 4—The Victory Debt

The most dangerous moment in health is not failure. It is early success.

You hit a milestone. The scale moves. Your blood pressure improves. Your jeans fit again. Your energy is back. And your brain—quietly, invisibly—declares victory. Standards soften. Tracking disappears. A few workouts get skipped. Nothing collapses immediately, so the drift continues. Then one day you look up and you are back where you started, paying the Pain Tax again.

This is not weakness. It is neuroscience. The brain's reward system registers the milestone as completion. The perceived need for effort drops. Behavior regresses toward the mean.

I call this the Victory Debt—every milestone creates a temporary drop in perceived urgency that makes regression feel safe. The CEO move is to pay the debt immediately by setting the next micro-target before the dopamine from the current win fades.

The protocol is simple: within 24 hours of hitting any milestone, name the next one. Not a bigger goal—the next specific, measurable commitment. Victory is a checkpoint, not a finish line. The system does not stop running because you had a good week.

> *Confidence after a win is the most predictable entry point for drift. Plan for it before it arrives.*

Winning Is Not the Same as Knowing How to Keep It

When it comes to weight loss—whether through discipline, surgery, or medication—I do not judge anyone's path. What matters is not how you lose the weight. What matters is whether you understand how to manage what comes after.

Here is the truth most programs never say out loud: if you do not understand the system you changed, the result will not last.

Lottery winners who lose their winnings don't fail because they're reckless—they fail because they were never taught how to manage money at that level. The system that produced the result was never explained to them. Health works the same way. If you don't understand what changed, you can't protect it.

I have seen people achieve extraordinary results through weight-loss surgery or medication. I have also seen just as many return to the same habits that created the problem in the first place. That is not failure of character. It is failure of education. The process gave them the win without teaching them how to operate differently once they had it.

The hard part of transformation is not losing the weight. It is learning how to lead yourself afterward. The body changes faster than the mindset. Without a system for managing the new normal, the old defaults reassert themselves. Not because the person is weak—because the system that produced the old behavior was never replaced with a better one.

Health is not a one-time transaction. It is an ongoing operating system that requires literacy, structure, and governance. You would not hand your company to someone who does not understand finance. Do not hand your health to a quick fix without understanding how to sustain what it produces.

Whether you are taking the long road of habit change or using medical intervention, the rule is the same: know your why, manage your wins, and build systems that keep you accountable long after the excitement fades.

> *If you do not understand how to manage health, you will lose it—no matter how you got it.*

> *Speed without stewardship is a gamble. And the house always wins.*

You Do Not Need Twelve New Habits. You Need One That Pulls the Rest.

The most successful companies do not rely on Hail Mary moves. They rely on repeatable systems—small, consistent processes that compound over time into something nobody can easily replicate.

Too many people approach health the same way they approach New Year's resolutions: twelve new habits at once, all starting Monday. By the following Sunday, nine of them are gone and the guilt from losing the nine has made dropping the remaining three feel inevitable.

Behavioral research has identified what author James Clear—in his book Atomic Habits—calls a keystone habit: a single core behavior that, when consistent, pulls other behaviors into formation.

For me, that keystone is my 5 a.m. workout. Not because it burns the most calories or builds the most muscle. Because it is the first thing I do for myself—before the phone starts, before the demands stack up, before the day has opinions about where my energy goes.

When I take care of myself first, I have something to give everyone else. The system orients the day before the day has a chance to orient me. My nutrition choices are sharper. My focus holds longer. I show up differently for my family, my work, and the people who need something from me.

If that session gets skipped, I feel it everywhere. Not just physically—in how I lead the rest of the day. That is how you know you have found your keystone. It is not the hardest habit. It is the one that makes every other habit possible.

The test for a keystone habit is simple: when this one behavior is in place, does the rest of the system run better? If yes, protect it above everything else. It is the load-bearing wall. Do not renovate the room by removing it.

To install a keystone habit, attach it to something you already do without thinking—a behavior so embedded in your daily structure that it happens automatically. Stretching while the coffee brews. A ten-minute walk immediately after lunch. Reviewing your KPIs the moment you sit down at your desk Monday morning. The new behavior borrows the consistency of the old one.

Once the keystone is stable—meaning you have executed it at least 20 of 30 days—add one supporting habit. Not five. One. Build the system the way you would build a company: foundational infrastructure first, then expansion.

Bryan Johnson Spends Millions Not to Die. You Have a Better Option.

Bryan Johnson, the tech entrepreneur featured on 60 Minutes and CNN, has built his entire identity around one mission: do not die. He spends millions annually, follows a six-hour daily health protocol, and takes over 100 supplements in pursuit of reversing his biological age. His results are remarkable—lab tests suggest the heart of a man in his 30s, the lungs of someone younger.

His commitment is real. His results are real. And his model is completely unreplicable for 99.9 percent of the people reading this book.

Here is what he actually proves, if you look past the extraordinary specifics: longevity responds to systems. Not genetics, not luck, not a single intervention. Systems. Consistent inputs, tracked over time, adjusted with precision, never abandoned because motivation dipped.

You do not need six hours a day. You do not need 100 supplements or a medical team running your bloodwork weekly. What you need is the principle behind the protocol: an operating model you can run for the rest of your life—sustainable, scalable, and honest about what your actual schedule and resources can support.

Longevity does not require millions. It requires daily movement you can sustain. Meals you can repeat without decision fatigue. Sleep that genuinely restores you. Routines that fit inside the realities of work, family, and a full life. If you cannot maintain it at 80, it is not the right plan. It is just a more expensive version of the Sprint Trap.

The Scale Is a Lagging Indicator. Stop Running Your Life on a Lagging Indicator.

The scale is the most commonly used and most misleading health metric available. It measures one output—total body weight—and tells you nothing about what is actually changing inside the system.

Muscle is denser than fat. When you build muscle and lose fat simultaneously—which is exactly what quality training and nutrition produce—the scale can sit still or move upward while your body composition improves dramatically. The scale reports a neutral quarter while the underlying business is posting record performance.

The CEO move is to measure the leading indicators—the inputs and early-signal outputs that predict where the system is heading, not just where it has been. Run these alongside the scale:

- Body measurements: chest, waist, arms, thighs. These often move when the scale does not.
- Energy stability: Are you crashing in the afternoon? That is a metabolic signal, not a motivation problem.
- Sleep quality: Restoring or not? HRV trending up or down?
- Strength trajectory: Are you moving more weight or more reps than last month?
- Adherence rate: How many commitments did you keep this week versus how many you set? That percentage is your real score.

Adherence rate is the most important metric in sustainable health. Not because it feels motivational—but because it is honest. It measures the gap between intention and execution—the exact gap that determines whether a plan survives long term.

Individuals who track their behavior and set specific goals are 76 percent more likely to maintain their health routine at the 12-month mark.[2] The Operating Sheet is not busywork. It is your 76 percent.

In EHOS terms, adherence rate is the Review step made honest. It does not ask how well you performed. It asks whether you showed up for the loop at all. A system that gets reviewed—even imperfectly—outperforms a perfect system that never gets checked.

Track it weekly. Set a target—80 percent is a high-performing operating standard, not a consolation prize. An athlete who executes 80 percent of a well-designed plan will outperform one who executes a perfect plan 40 percent of the time. Consistency beats intensity. Every. Single. Time.

> *You cannot manage what you do not measure. But you also cannot sustain what you are afraid to measure honestly.*

Before I share how this works in my own life, I want to name something the chapter has not said directly yet. When the system drifts, the people around you notice before you do. Not because they are watching the scale. Because they feel the version of you that shows up when the operating model is not running.

That is the real cost of drift—and the real reason the architecture in this chapter matters.

Let me tell you what this actually looks like in my life. I am not exempt from any of this. I face the same pressures every executive in this book faces—travel schedules that compress sleep, long flights where convenience food is the only option, weeks where the agenda runs the day instead of the other way around.

My 5 a.m. crew workouts are not about intensity. They are about accountability. When I show up, my crew shows up. That social contract makes consistency easier than motivation ever could. But travel breaks that contract. And when it breaks, I have learned to make deals—not perfect decisions, deals. I protect sleep on long flights more aggressively than I protect my diet. I prep snacks before trips specifically so the airport does not make my food decisions for me.

And weight? I have a number. When the scale gets within range of 200 pounds, I do not spiral. I start tracking my food again. That is it. No dramatic restart. No punishment. Just one specific behavior that I already know works, re-engaged until the number moves back to where I want it. That is the system.

I did not restart. I re-entered. That is not a small distinction. Starting over requires motivation. Re-entering just requires executing the next rep. The tools in this chapter are not theory. They are what I use when the system I teach breaks down in my own life. And they were designed—specifically, architecturally—so that when it happens to you, you do not have to figure out what to do. You just have to do the thing you already decided.

I am the expert in my own life. Not because I never fall short. Because when I do, I know exactly what to do next.

1. Build your three-element operating model before this week ends. One sentence for your Minimum Standard. One sentence for your Operating Rhythm. One pre-decided threshold for your Relapse Trigger Reset.
2. Define your Danger Zone thresholds for each domain—weight, training, sleep, nutrition, energy—on Operating Sheet 9. Write them now, when you are thinking clearly, so you do not have to think clearly when you are in the Danger Zone. Pre-decided beats in-the-moment. Every time.
3. Identify your keystone habit—the one behavior that, when locked in, pulls the rest of the system into formation. Install it by attaching it to something you already do automatically. Execute it for 30 days before adding anything else. The system is built in reps, not intentions.

EXECUTIVE DEBRIEF

"Most people do not fail at health because they lack commitment. They fail because they built a plan that was never designed to last."

Complete this Operating Sheet in the book, or log your answers directly into the EHOS Dashboard at adrianmwilliams.com. Members with a free account can access all worksheets, save their responses by chapter, and generate their CEO of Me Health Resume automatically from their answers.

Executive Action 1—Your Operating Model: Minimum Standard (one sentence—the floor, not the goal): _________________ Operating Rhythm (your default weekly cadence): _________________
Relapse Trigger Reset (pre-decided threshold + what you do):
____

Executive Action 2—Your Danger Zone Thresholds:
Weight: _________________ Training: _________________
Sleep: _________________ Nutrition: _________________
Energy: _________________

Executive Action 3—Your Keystone Habit:
The one behavior: _________________ What it attaches to (existing habit): _________________ 30-day start date: _________________

Congratulations—You've Earned These Skills

Health Retention Architect—Designed a three-element operating model—Minimum Standard, Operating Rhythm, and Relapse Trigger Reset—that sustains execution through disruption by removing improvisation from the moment the system breaks down.

Failure Mode Risk Manager—Diagnosed and mitigated the four primary health sustainability failure modes—Sprint Trap, Danger Zone, 24-Hour Rule, and Victory Debt—deploying pre-decided system-level responses that remove emotion from high-pressure recovery moments.

HEALTH ADHERENCE ANALYST—MEASURED AND MANAGED WEEKLY HEALTH COMMITMENT ADHERENCE AS THE PRIMARY SUSTAINABILITY KPI, REPLACING SCALE-DEPENDENT PROGRESS TRACKING WITH LEADING-INDICATOR EXECUTION MONITORING THAT SURFACES PROBLEMS BEFORE THEY COMPOUND.

SOM Element	Write Yours Here
Minimum Standard (MS) One sentence. The least you will do on your hardest week.	___________________________ ___________________________
Operating Rhythm (OR) Your non-negotiable weekly cadence. What runs automatically.	Monday: _______________ Thursday: _____________ Daily anchor behavior: _____________________
Relapse Trigger Reset (RTR) Weight threshold:	If scale reads ______ for ______ consecutive days: __________ ___________________________
Relapse Trigger Reset (RTR) Training threshold:	If I miss ______ consecutive sessions: ________________ ___________________________
Relapse Trigger Reset (RTR) Sleep threshold:	If sleep drops below ______ hrs for ______ nights: _________ ___________________________
Relapse Trigger Reset (RTR) Nutrition threshold:	If SIS baseline breaks for ______ consecutive days: ________ ___________________________
Universal reset protocol (same every time)	Step 1 Stabilize: ________________________ Step 2 Simplify: ________________________ Step 3 Execute: ________________________

Domain	Your Healthy Operating Standard	Danger Zone Threshold (pre-decided, non-negotiable)	Reset Protocol
Weight	e.g. 185 lbs	e.g. +8 lbs for 5+ days	Return to SIS baseline and daily movement
Training	e.g. 4 sessions/week	e.g. 3 missed days in a row	Execute minimum standard next morning. No negotiation.
Sleep	e.g. 7 hrs avg	e.g. Under 6 hrs for 4+ nights	Protect bedtime window. Cut one evening commitment.
Nutrition	e.g. SIS baseline meals	e.g. 4+ consecutive non-SIS days	Rebuild one SIS meal today. Not tomorrow. Today.
Energy / Mood	e.g. Productive by 9am	e.g. Afternoon crash 5+ days in a row	Audit sleep, nutrition, and hydration first.

Step 1: Stabilize   Return to:_________________________________

Step 2: Simplify   Remove: _________________________________

Step 3: Execute fundamentals   My non-negotiable first move is: _______________

Reflective Learning from Your Health Turnaround

You Are No Longer the Patient. You Are the Operator.

Nine chapters ago you opened this book looking for answers. You end it with something more durable than answers: a system.

Chapter 10 starts with a truth I learned the hard way.

After years of coaching clients and running my own health with the same discipline I bring to business, I noticed something that does not change. The breakdown is rarely random. It is patterned. Predictable. Almost identical from one person to the next.

For a long time, I thought my job was motivation. Get you fired up. Get you committed. Get you moving. But motivation is not the asset most people think it is. Motivation shows up for moments, not for life.

That realization changed my entire approach to training and coaching. Because the goal of great coaching is to put yourself out of business. If I do my job right, you should not need me forever. You should graduate. You should be able to run your own health with competence, clarity, and consistency—with or without anyone watching.

But here is what I kept seeing instead.

People did not want a lifestyle change. They wanted a moment change.

> *A wedding.*
> *A reunion.*
> *A vacation.*
> *A class photo.*
> *A deadline.*

For that moment, they will do whatever it takes. Wake up early. Lock in every meal. Hit every workout. Follow the plan like it is mission critical. Then the event happens. The pictures get posted. The compliments come.

And the discipline disappears.

Not because they are lazy. Not because they are broken. Because the system was never built for sustainability. It was built for a finish line. And a finish line is not a system. It is an exit.

Chapter 10 is about something different. It is about breaking that restart cycle—permanently. Not with another motivational push. Not with dependency on a coach or a program or a plan someone else designed.

With honest accountability. The kind that teaches you how to operate in the other 23 hours. The kind that turns a short-term push into a lifelong standard.

> *Your body does not reward what you promise. It rewards what you repeatedly deliver. You have now run every phase of EHOS—not in theory, but across nine chapters of real decisions, real pressure, and real execution. That is not a credential. That is proof.*

Coaching Only Works If It Turns Into Ownership

There is a pattern I have watched play out in corporate environments that looks almost identical to what I see in health. A company brings in a world-class consultant. The leadership team is energized. There are whiteboard sessions and strategy decks and off-site meetings. Everyone leaves aligned and inspired.

Then the consultant flies home.

And in the weeks that follow, nothing changes. The deck sits in a shared drive. The recommendations stay on slide 14. The daily operations continue exactly as they were before the engagement. The company spent real money, real time, and real attention—and implemented nothing.

This is not a story about a bad consultant. It is a story about a common and expensive mistake: confusing proximity with progress.

> *You did not buy transformation. You bought proximity. And proximity does not produce results. Execution does.*

Health has the same trap. And in my years of coaching, I have seen it play out the same way.

Some people approach support—a trainer, a nutritionist, a coach—the way they approach a credential. It is something to have, to mention, to signal. It looks responsible. It sounds committed. It can even feel like progress, because you showed up. You invested. You are taking it seriously.

But a coach is not a credential. A trainer is not an accessory. They are infrastructure. And infrastructure only works if you use it to build something that runs when they are not in the room.

The 23-Hour Standard

Here is the math that changes everything.

A nutritionist or a trainer may be with you 30 to 60 minutes. Therapy might run 45 minutes to an hour. That is the easy hour—the structured hour, the supported hour, the hour with someone watching.

Then you walk out the door. The coached hour is done. The other 23 belong entirely to you.

That is where outcomes are built.

If the only time you execute is when you are in the room with a professional, you do not have a program. You have a performance. You are performing health for an audience of one, and the moment that audience leaves, the performance ends.

The real question is not who your coach is. The real question is who you are when nobody is watching. Because your results are not built in the 60-minute session. They are built in the 23 hours that follow it.

This is why some people can have a coach for years and still not look coached. The support was real. The investment was real. But the ownership never transferred. The system never moved from the professional's hands into theirs.

Coaching only works if it turns into ownership. Not hype. Not a plan you follow only when someone is watching. A system that holds when life is normal—and still runs when life gets loud.

The Pain Tax in Execution Terms

The Pain Tax lands differently when you see it in your calendar. Here is what it costs in practice.

It is easier to stay in shape than it is to get in shape. It is easier to keep weight off than it is to take it off.

When your system is running—when your habits are locked, your standard is clear, and your protocols are in place—the daily investment is roughly 4 percent of your day. One hour out of twenty-four. Applied consistently, that fraction produces compounding returns that most people spend their entire lives chasing with approaches that cost them far more.

But when you drift, the comeback costs significantly more. In my years of coaching, I have watched the same pattern repeat without exception: the effort to rebuild is exponentially higher than the effort to maintain. More restriction than you ran before. More catch-up workouts on a body that is already behind. More mental bandwidth spent managing the gap between where you are and where you were. More of everything—while producing less, because you are rebuilding instead of compounding.

That is the Pain Tax expressed in execution terms. Not a philosophy—a calendar event. Deferred maintenance that accumulates quietly until the bill is larger than anyone planned to pay.

The solution is not harder discipline. The solution is a system that catches the drift before the tax compounds. That is what this chapter makes permanent.

Three Lessons That Show Up in Every Breakdown. Mine. My Clients'. The Industry's.

Over 30 years in corporate America and more than 30 years coaching clients across every fitness level, income bracket, and professional background, I have watched the same three breakdowns repeat. Not occasionally. Consistently. In my own health journey, in the people I coach, and in the patterns the industry keeps selling solutions for.

These are not theories I developed in a training room. They are lessons I paid tuition on personally, watched clients pay tuition on repeatedly, and observed the broader industry get wrong in ways that cost millions of people real time, real money, and real momentum.

Each one is a pattern you can now recognize—and route around—for the rest of your operating life.

Lesson 1: Charisma Is Not Credibility—This Built Chapter 7

I made this mistake myself early on. I followed fitness influencers who had large platforms, high energy, and zero clinical backing. I spent real money on supplements that did not deliver. Real time on protocols that were built for marketing, not metabolism. The results did not match the label—because the label was never written for me. It was written for a sale.

But I have watched the same pattern play out in clients far more often than it played out in me. Smart, capable, high-performing professionals who would never approve a vendor in a boardroom without reviewing credentials—but who completely abandon that filter the moment someone with a fitness following and a before-and-after photo tells them what they want to hear.

And the industry makes it worse. The fitness space is one of the least regulated professional environments that influences daily behavior at scale. A person can build an audience of millions, push a supplement line with no clinical trial behind it, and face no accountability when the results do not materialize. The incentive is to sell. The cost lands on you.

The lesson is the same whether it came from my experience, a client's, or the industry's track record: a large following is not a peer review. Confidence is not evidence. Charisma does not equal credibility. Until you demand receipts—peer-reviewed data, real-world outcomes, alignment with your own system—you are not making a health decision. You are making a marketing decision.

The Diagnostic First Rule is your filter now. Apply it to everything that comes at you—regardless of where it shows up.

Lesson 2: Grit Without Governance Is Controlled Demolition— This Built Chapters 6 and 9

I learned this one the hard way. When I trained for the Guinness World Record for the most push-ups in one hour, my daily volume was between 2,000 and 2,600 push-ups for eight consecutive months. On the day of the attempt, I tore my rotator cuff around push-up 300 without realizing it. I pushed through. I finished with just under 1,200 push-ups in the hour. The record did not fall. My shoulder paid the bill.

What that experience taught me—and what I have since watched clients repeat in their own ways—is that discipline without a governance structure is not strength. It is a liability dressed up as commitment. You can be completely dedicated, showing up every day, doing everything right by surface appearance, and still be building toward a breakdown because there is no system checking the signals.

I see this in clients who overtrain for events and arrive at race day already depleted. I see it in executives who white-knuckle a nutrition protocol for 90 days and then collapse into the exact behaviors they were trying to eliminate—because the system was built for intensity, not sustainability. And I see it across the industry in programs that celebrate volume and suffering as proof of commitment, with no recovery architecture, no threshold triggers, and no off-ramp when the body starts sending signals it cannot afford to keep ignoring.

Grit is real. It matters. But grit without governance does not produce durability. It produces a delayed breakdown—and the delay is what makes it dangerous, because by the time the cost shows up, the investment is already too deep to easily exit.

The 3-Try Rule, the Obstacle Removal Protocol, the Sprint Trap threshold, the Relapse Trigger Reset—every one of those tools exists to catch what pure discipline misses. You have them installed. Use them.

Lesson 3: You Cannot Outsource Your 23 Hours—This Built the Entire EHOS

I speak to people every day who are still living this pattern. A client invests in a coach, a program, or a plan. They show up for the session. They execute when someone is watching. Their results in that window are real. But the coached hour is one hour. The other 23 belong entirely to them—and most have no system governing that time. The session was never the problem. The unstructured hours that follow it are.

The pattern I have watched destroy otherwise disciplined people is always the same. A client invests in a coach, a program, or a platform. They show up for the session. They execute while supervised. Then the program ends—and without the external structure, the behavior collapses because ownership was never built. They paid for proximity to expertise without doing the harder work of internalizing the system. It took watching real losses—time, money, physical setbacks—before I understood that no professional, no matter how skilled, can govern your 23 hours for you. That realization is what built EHOS.

What finally changed everything—for me and for the clients I have watched make this shift—was treating health the way I had spent over 30 years treating enterprise systems in corporate America. With baselines. Audits. Documented protocols. A feedback loop that caught problems before they compounded into crises. Not reacting to the environment. Governing it.

When you make that shift—from customer to operator, from dependent to self-governing—the results change permanently. Not because you found a better program. Because you stopped needing one. You became the program.

The system is now yours. Run it.

If these three lessons were filed as a business case study, the executive summary would read:

Root cause: Outsourced judgment. Confused effort with governance. Paid the Pain Tax late—in setbacks, restarts, and lost time—instead of early in discipline and structure.

Pattern: Consistent across individual experience, client history, and industry behavior. The breakdown is rarely random. It is always a system failure presenting as a personal failure.

Intervention: Install the operating system. Establish the baseline. Build the governance architecture. Move ownership of the 23 hours from the environment into your own hands.

Result: A system that runs on standards instead of motivation—and self-corrects before drift becomes default.

The variable was never talent. Never genetics. Never finding the right coach or the right program. It was the decision to stop being a customer of your own health and become the operator of it.

You have already made that decision. That is why you are here.

> *Once you understand the process—what works, what doesn't, and why—you can always return to your peak. That knowledge cannot be taken from you. It is the only asset that compounds without limit.*

This Is What Ten Chapters Built. This Is What You Are Now Running.

Step back and look at what you actually built.

Not a plan. Not a program. Not a collection of wellness tips stacked into chapters. An operating system. The Executive Health Operating System—EHOS. Ten phases. Ten chapters. One integrated framework that runs on standards instead of motivation, on data instead of hope, and on governance instead of willpower.

This is not a system you picked up. It is a system you built. That distinction matters enormously. You understand why every component exists. You know what connects to what. You know what breaks first when it goes missing. That means you can rebuild any part of it, at any point, without starting from scratch.

EHOS Phase	Chapter	What You Built	Signature Concept
AUDIT	Ch 1	Health Portfolio + Baseline	Pain Tax
STRATEGY	Ch 2	Vision, Mission, Turnaround Blueprint	Health Mission Statement
EXECUTION	Ch 3	Daily SOPs + Minimum Viable Day	Minimum Standard
INVESTMENT	Ch 4	ROI Filter + Capital Allocation	Pain Tax: Early vs. Late
GOVERNANCE	Ch 5	Personal Health Board	Board Seat Architecture
SUSTAINABILITY	Ch 6	Execution Loop + Friction Removal	3-Try Rule
INNOVATION	Ch 7	Signal Filter + R&D Sprint	Diagnostic First Rule
BRANDING	Ch 8	Health Identity + Private Wins	Non-Negotiable Standard
RETENTION	Ch 9	SOM + Danger Zone Thresholds	Relapse Trigger Reset
REFLECTION	Ch 10	Audit/Adapt/Lead Loop	Annual Health Case Study

Every row in that table is a decision already made. When the pressure arrives, the system answers.

Every concept in that table was designed to replace a reaction with a standard. That is the only thing a system actually does—it converts decisions you used to make under pressure into decisions that are already made. The pressure arrives. The system answers.

Three Principles That Govern Everything From Here

Simplicity: If it is too complex to execute on your worst week, it will not survive your worst month. Every time you are tempted to add a layer, ask whether the layer serves the mission or serves the feeling of doing more. Complexity is the enemy of consistency.

Sustainability: If you cannot do it at age 70, 80, or 90, it is not a system. It is a season. The Guinness attempt was a season. The 90-day challenge is a season. A system built for the arc of your life looks completely different from a program built for a moment. Build for the arc.

Alignment: If it does not serve your mission, cut it. Not reduce it. Cut it. Every habit, every commitment, every tool must pass through this filter before it earns a place in your operating model. The system is only as clean as what you refuse to add to it.

> *You are not managing symptoms anymore. You are managing a system. That changes everything about what is possible from here.*

Audit. Adapt. Lead. The Loop That Never Stops Running.

One habit separates health leaders from health restarters. Not a framework. Not a tool. A cadence. A loop that converts every setback into a diagnosis and every drift into a course correction—before it becomes a crisis.

The loop has three movements. They are not sequential steps you run once. They are a permanent operating rhythm—weekly, monthly, quarterly, for the rest of your life.

Audit: Stop guessing. Start tracking. Weekly and monthly check-ins on your meals, energy, habits, sleep, and training surface what is working and what is drifting. Your body tells the truth. The data makes sure you hear it before the bill compounds.

Adapt: Health is not static. Life shifts—career transitions, family demands, seasonal changes, unexpected setbacks. When the environment changes, you pivot with intention, not panic. Rigid plans shatter under real life. Governed systems absorb it and return to baseline.

Lead: Show up consistently. You do not need perfection to lead—you need alignment between your standard and your behavior. When those two things match, something changes in the people around you. They see that it is possible. Whether they say so or not, it recalibrates what they believe is available to them.

Use this loop coming off your best month or crawling out of your hardest season. Do not spiral. Do not start over. Do not wait for Monday. Run the loop. Audit what happened. Adapt one thing. Lead the next rep.

> *The loop does not require a perfect week. It requires an honest one.*

The Holiday Protocol—Applied Leadership Under Predictable Pressure

Every year I have the same conversation with clients. Someone says the holidays snuck up on them.

I say: it is the same date it was last year. It did not sneak. You did not plan.

Predictable disruptions are not disruptions. They are calendar events. The executive who treats Q4 as a surprise every year does not have a planning problem. They have a governance problem. Same principle applies here.

One of my clients hosts a large holiday dinner every year. The food abundance has always been a challenge—not because he lacks discipline, but because the environment is engineered to overwhelm individual decision-making. The protocol is simpler than you might expect: decide your standard before you sit down, not after the second plate. A smaller portion of what's there. A slower pace. One plate, not three. And the next morning, you return to your standard—no spiral, no shame, slightly more movement if you want to balance the ledger. The system absorbs real life. That is exactly the point.

And if it goes sideways anyway—you adjust the next day. Slightly reduced intake. A few extra minutes of movement. No spiral. No shame. No fresh-start speech. The system absorbs real life and returns to baseline. That is what a governed system does that willpower alone never can.

Every holiday. Every work sprint. Every season of life that has knocked you off course before—it is already on the calendar. Plan for it before it arrives. That is the CEO standard applied to your own operations.

> *Life does not just happen. It unfolds according to how well you prepared.*

SECTION 5 — CLOSING THE LOOP

You Are Not Just Building This for Yourself

There is a concept in business that rarely gets discussed until the end of a career, and by then it is often too late to act on it with full intention. Legacy. Not the monument kind. The operational kind. The knowledge, the systems, the standards you leave behind that allow the next generation to start from a higher floor than you did.

The most durable family businesses are not the ones that made the most money. They are the ones that transferred the process. The founders did not just build revenue—they documented the system, instilled the values, and made sure that when they stepped back, the enterprise could run without them because everyone around them had been trained to operate at the same standard.

Your health works exactly the same way.

Here is what nobody tells you about health decline. It is not a private experience.

The afternoon crashes affect your decisions, and your decisions affect your team. The sleep debt affects your patience, and your patience affects every relationship you are in.

The slow erosion of capacity is visible to everyone around you long before you see it yourself.

Most people experience the cost of their own health failure as a personal problem. The people who love them and work with them experience it as a leadership problem.

You becoming the CEO of your health is not just a gift to yourself. It is a gift to every person who depends on your full capacity.

When you manage your health like a CEO—with a baseline, a mission, a board, execution protocols, and a reflection cadence—you do not just change your own trajectory. You change the trajectory of everyone watching you. The children in your household. The colleagues who see how you operate. The people you lead at work and in your community. They do not inherit your money when you are gone. They inherit your habits, your standards, and your example. That is the real estate that compounds across generations.

Most people receive a health inheritance they did not choose. Patterns passed down not through intention but through observation. What the family ate. How stress was managed. Whether doctors were visited regularly or only in crisis. Whether the body was treated as an asset or ignored until it became a liability.

You are breaking that chain. Not dramatically. Systematically.

Every time you execute your Minimum Standard on a hard week, someone sees it. Every time you make a food decision based on your SIS baseline instead of convenience, someone learns that it is possible. Every time you run your monthly review instead of drifting past the warning signs, you are modeling the behavior that your children, your family, and your community will carry long after this book is on a shelf.

My vision for my own health has never been just about me. It is longevity with purpose. Strong, clear-headed, present. I want to lead in my family, my business, and my community—not just through what I say, but through how I show up every single day. That standard—how I show up—is the real product of everything this book has built.

Sweat equity cannot be outsourced. No one can run your miles, make your food decisions, or install your governance cadence for you. That is the hardest truth in this entire book and also its greatest gift. Because it means the result is entirely yours. The person you become through this process—disciplined, data-driven, self-aware, resilient—belongs to you in a way that no shortcut, no supplement, and no program can replicate.

And when the people around you see it—when your children see a parent who does not negotiate with their health, who shows up consistently and governs themselves with the same seriousness they bring to work—they internalize a different story about what is possible. One that has nothing to do with willpower or genetics or finding the right motivation. One that is about systems. Standards. And the daily decision to lead yourself before you lead anyone else.

I wake up at 5 a.m. every day. Not because I am a morning person. Not because I love the dark. Because nothing happens at 5 a.m. except emergencies—and emergencies cannot be scheduled.

That hour belongs entirely to me. Before the phone starts. Before the demands stack up. Before the day has opinions about where my energy goes. I protect that hour the way a CEO protects the budget line that funds everything else—because that is exactly what it is.

What my kids have seen is not the workout. They have seen the discipline. The consistency. The fact that I show up for myself before I show up for anyone else—and because of that, I have more to give when they need it.

I can leave my children wealth. I have thought about this carefully. But if they do not have the health to spend it—the energy to enjoy it, the clarity to steward it, the longevity to watch it grow—then what exactly did I leave them?

The greatest inheritance is not in an account. It is in a standard. The standard that says: you take care of your body first, not last. Not when you have time. Not when things settle down. Before the day has a chance to talk you out of it.

That is what I am building. Not just for me. For the generation that comes after me—and the one after that.

> *The greatest gift you can give the people who come after you is not money. It is a model. Show them what it looks like to lead your health the way a CEO leads an enterprise—with clarity, discipline, and a system built to last.*

Gratitude is not a feeling you wait for. It is a decision you make about what the capacity you have built is for.

There is one more layer to this that the book has not named until now.

The veteran in Chapter 3—the man on the power tower, doing pull-ups for his three fallen brothers—was not training for himself. He was training for something larger than his own numbers. His WHY had a name, a face, a reason that outlasted any bad morning.

At some point in your health journey, the mission expands. It stops being just about your KPIs, your capacity, your numbers. It starts being about what you can do for others because of your capacity.

Running a race for a cause that matters to you. Training alongside your child because they need to see it is possible. Showing up for a colleague who is struggling, not with advice, but with an invitation.

The system you built is yours. The impact of the system extends to everyone in your orbit. That is not an obligation. It is the most powerful ROI the health operating system produces—and it compounds in ways no wearable will ever measure.

You did not just read a book.

For the rest of your life.

Consistently.

Not perfectly.

Now run it.

The system is yours. The impact extends far beyond you.

It is for the person you hand this book to one day—a child, a colleague, a friend who is struggling—and you say: this one changed how I operate.

It is for the team that gets the full version of you, not the depleted one.

It is for the people in your household who are watching and learning what is possible—not from what you say, but from what you do before the day begins.

It is for the version of you that shows up at 70, at 80—still moving, still present, still building something worth leaving.

Now here is what that work is really for.

Not because you were given it. Because you did the work.

You built all of that. And it belongs entirely to you.

A baseline that replaced guessing. A strategy that survived your real calendar. An operating system that runs when motivation does not show up. A board that holds the standard when you cannot. A brand built in private wins nobody applauded. A retention architecture designed from the start never to fail. A reflection cadence that turns every setback into a lesson and every lesson into a stronger system.

You built something.

THREE ACTION STEPS

1. Run your Annual Health Debrief on Operating Sheet 10.1 within the next seven days. Not at the new year. Not when things settle down. Now—while the system is fresh and the clarity is highest. Answer all eight questions honestly. Set three health KPIs for the next twelve months. Lock in next year's debrief date before you close the sheet.
2. Install the Audit/Adapt/Lead cadence on Operating Sheet 10.2. Assign a specific day and time to your weekly ten-minute check-in. Block your monthly strategy review. Schedule your quarterly portfolio audit. These are board meetings. Treat them with the same discipline you give your most critical professional commitments.
3. Identify one person in your life—a child, a partner, a colleague— who would benefit from seeing one standard you keep. Not a lecture. A model. Decide this week what you will do consistently, in front of them, without announcement. The system starts with you. The impact extends well beyond you.

EXECUTIVE DEBRIEF

You came into this book with a body you were managing by feel.

You leave it with a system.

Not a plan someone designed for you. Not a program you will follow until the motivation runs out. A system you built—phase by phase, chapter by chapter—that runs on standards instead of feelings, on governance instead of willpower, and on design instead of discipline alone.

The EHOS loop never stops. It does not need you to be perfect. It needs you to return. Every week. Every month. Every year. That return—consistent, honest, unglamorous—is the only thing that separates a health story from a health operating system.

You are the operator now. Act like it.

"Nine chapters ago you opened this book looking for answers. You end it with something more durable: a system that belongs to you, runs on your standards, and self-corrects for the rest of your life."

OPERATING SHEET 10.1

Annual Health Debrief—Your Yearly Case Study Review

Purpose: Extract the truth from the last twelve months. Carry the best of it forward. Make the next year better than the last.

Cadence: Once per year. Same date. Non-negotiable. Set next year's date before closing this sheet.

Figure 10.2 *Annual Health Debrief — Case Study Review Template*

Debrief Question	Your Answer
What was my single biggest health win this year?	
What was the root cause of my biggest breakdown?	
Which system performed best under pressure?	
Which system failed first when life got loud?	
What did I keep doing that I should have stopped?	
What did I stop doing that I should have kept?	
What is the one upgrade I carry into the next year?	
What is my health vision or the next 3 years?	

Forward Planning	Your Commitment
Three health KPIs for the next 12 months:	1. __________________________ 2. __________________________ 3. __________________________
The one system that needs the most attention:	__________________________
Date of next year's Annual Health Debrief:	__________________________

Operating Sheet 10.2

Audit / Adapt / Lead—Your Permanent Review Cadence

Purpose: Install the governance loop that makes every layer of your health system self-correcting for life.

Cadence	Duration	Questions to Answer
Weekly Executive Check-in	10 min Same day each week	What drifted? What is my single correction? What is my minimum standard this week?
Monthly Strategy Review	20 min First Monday of month	Are KPIs trending correctly? What habit costs the most energy? What needs to be funded or cut?
Quarterly Portfolio Audit	30 min End of each quarter	What worked? Double down. What failed? Cut or redesign. What risk needs attention before it compounds?
Annual Health Case Study	60 min Same date every year	Run the full Annual Debrief. Update EHOS phase status. Set three KPIs for the next 12 months.

My Committed Cadence	Day / Time / Location
Weekly Executive Check-in (10 min)	__________________________
Monthly Strategy Review (20 min)	__________________________
Quarterly Portfolio Audit (30 min)	__________________________
Annual Health Debrief (60 min)	__________________________
Next scheduled physical:	__________________________

Congratulations—You've Earned These Skills

Health Performance Reviewer—Established a structured weekly, monthly, quarterly, and annual health review cadence, extracting pattern intelligence, catching drift before it compounds, and driving continuous system improvement through honest self-assessment.

Health System Adapter—Applied the Audit-Adapt-Lead loop to convert every setback, life transition, and environmental shift into a structured system adjustment, maintaining strategic continuity without rigid adherence to conditions that no longer exist.

Health Legacy Builder—Established a visible, consistent health operating standard that models executive-level self-governance for family, colleagues, and community, converting personal health discipline into generational leadership infrastructure.

Ten chapters. One operating system.

Built by you. Governed by you. Running on your standards.

You did not just read this book.

You built an operating system.

You replaced guesswork with governance.

You replaced motivation with standards.

You replaced starting over with the ability to re-enter.

And everything you have built—every standard you keep,

every rep you execute, every system you run —

is being watched by someone who needs to see it is possible.

You are the CEO of your health.

You are the model.

You are the legacy in progress.

Now lead accordingly.

Chief Executive Officer—You, Inc.

Health, Performance & Longevity Division | Term: Lifetime | Reports To: Reality

PREPARED FOR: ______________________________

EXECUTIVE SUMMARY

Health leader with a complete 10-phase Executive Health Operating System (EHOS) governing audit, strategy, execution, investment, governance, sustainability, innovation, branding, retention, and reflection. Demonstrated ability to build, manage, and sustain personal health as a high-performance enterprise. Operates by system, not by motivation. Governed by data, not by trend.

CORE COMPETENCIES

- **Health Portfolio Management:** Audits health assets and liabilities using executive KPI frameworks; replaces guesswork with data-driven baselines
- **Strategic Planning & Mission Design:** Authors long-term health vision and SWOT-driven strategy with 30/60/90-day execution benchmarks
- **Systems Execution:** Builds and deploys SOPs for nutrition, movement, sleep, and recovery that run without relying on motivation
- **Capital Allocation & ROI Filtering:** Screens health investments against KPI-tied return criteria using Pain Tax framework; eliminates low-value spend
- **Board Governance & Accountability:** Assembles and chairs a Personal Health Board of Directors; institutes weekly, monthly, and quarterly review cadences
- **Sustainability & Risk Management:** Defines Danger Zone thresholds and Relapse Trigger Resets; governs the 24-Hour Rule and Victory Debt protocols
- **Innovation & Diagnostic Leadership:** Runs quarterly health R&D sprints; filters technology adoption through a three-criteria ROI governance model

- **Identity & Brand Alignment:** Operates from identity-first habit architecture; executes Brand Gap Scans to align behavior with stated standards
- **Reflective Leadership & Legacy:** Runs Annual Health Case Study reviews; deploys Audit/Adapt/Lead loop as permanent governance cadence
- **Contingency & Disruption Planning:** Pre-writes If/Then/Else protocols for travel, pressure seasons, and calendar-predictable disruptions

Chief Reflection Officer—Health Reflection Division | Chapter 10
Closed the EHOS loop; installed permanent governance cadence and generational legacy standard

- Deployed Audit/Adapt/Lead loop as the permanent operating cadence across all EHOS phases
- Executed Annual Health Debrief protocol; extracted pattern intelligence and set forward KPIs
- Engineered pre-built Holiday Protocol and disruption plans for all calendar-predictable pressure events
- Established generational health legacy standard—visible, consistent model for family and community

Chief Retention Officer—Health Sustainability Division | Chapter 9
Designed failure-proof operating model; deployed four-mode breakdown prevention system

- Built Sustainable Operating Model: Minimum Standard, Operating Rhythm, Relapse Trigger Reset
- Defined Danger Zone thresholds across all key health domains with pre-decided reset protocols
- Applied 24-Hour Rule to separate execution misses from identity, preventing spiral regression
- Diagnosed and mitigated Victory Debt—the drift window that follows early success

Chief Brand Officer—Personal Health Brand Division | Chapter 8
Defined health identity; aligned daily behavior to stated standards through Brand Gap protocols

- Defined personal health brand: three core identity words, three non-negotiable standards

- Executed Brand Gap Scan; diagnosed behavior-identity misalignment and built realignment plan
- Installed identity-first habit architecture replacing effort-based behavior change
- Applied Constraint Rebrand framework to sustain mission during setback and life disruption

Chief Innovation Officer—Health Technology & Diagnostics Division | Chapter 7

Governed health technology adoption; ran controlled experimentation against fixed KPI baselines

- Instituted quarterly Background Update cadence to compound improvements without reactive overhauls
- Implemented diagnostic-first protocol: data before prescription, signal before solution
- Built Health KPI Stack—one primary scoreboard with supporting metrics separating signal from noise
- Deployed stress-resilient breach containment: detect, downshift, protect minimum standard

Chief Sustainability Officer—Health Resilience Division | Chapter 6

Built execution systems that survive real life; removed friction before it became behavioral drift

- Defined and enforced Minimum Standard—floor-level execution for high-stress and disrupted weeks
- Applied Obstacle Removal Protocol: named friction, reduced barriers, assigned board accountability
- Deployed 3-Try Decision Framework to evaluate new habits before keeping, modifying, or cutting
- Redesigned environment defaults and social occasion protocols to reinforce mission alignment

Chief Governance Officer—Personal Health Board Division | Chapter 5

Assembled and governed Personal Health Board; installed decision rights and board review cadence

- Recruited governance Chair with explicit authority to enforce non-negotiables and flag drift
- Assigned board seats by verified competence; separated professional from independent director roles
- Engineered relapse risk controls: trigger identification, boundary enforcement,

Chief Investment Officer—Health Capital Division　| 　Chapter 4

Reallocated health resources using ROI framework; deployed Pain Tax prevention strategy

- Screened every health investment against KPI-tied return criteria; eliminated low-value spending
- Applied Pain Tax framework to address known liabilities before compounding into lost capacity
- Launched SIS Fuel System: tiered nutrition governance across all conditions and schedules
- Engineered Executive Health KPI Dashboard tracking inputs, outputs, and leading risk indicators

Chief Operations Officer—Health Execution Division　| 　Chapter 3

Built and deployed repeatable daily health SOPs across nutrition, movement, sleep, and recovery

- Defined Minimum Viable Day: floor-level execution standard for high-pressure, low-resource days
- Deployed Single Ingredient Standard (SIS): binary nutrition rule eliminating hidden liabilities
- Pre-wrote If/Then/Else contingency protocols for travel, schedule disruption, and real-life variance
- Embedded non-negotiable health behaviors into calendar infrastructure as locked commitments

Chief Strategy Officer—Health Mission & Planning Division　| Chapter 2

Converted audit findings into a governed long-term health strategy with KPIs and accountability

- Authored personal health vision, mission statement, and SWOT-driven strategic plan
- Engineered milestone-sequenced goal architecture with 30/60/90-day performance benchmarks
- Architected change management systems to pre-empt resistance, friction, and schedule disruption
- Constructed review cadences and governance standards that sustain execution without motivation

Chief Audit Officer—Health Portfolio & Baseline Division | Chapter 1

Health Portfolio Analyst—Conducted a full baseline audit across six health domains using objective data and a personal SWOT framework, replacing emotional self-assessment with evidence-based executive decision-making.

- Health Baseline Architect—Established measurable starting-point KPIs across strength, sleep, nutrition, and recovery to create a data foundation that supports every subsequent strategic and operational health decision.
- Health Risk Identifier—Diagnosed personal health liabilities and early-warning signals before they became operational failures, converting reactive crisis management into proactive risk governance.

PERFORMANCE METRICS—KPI BASELINE

- **EHOS Phases Activated:** 10 of 10
- **Total Skills Earned: 30 across 10 chapters**
- **Annual Health Debrief:** Scheduled: _______________________________
- **Weekly Check-in Cadence:** Day / Time: _______________________________
- **Primary Health KPI (Year 1):** _______________________________
- **Danger Zone Threshold (Weight):** _______________________________
- **Next Annual Physical:** _______________________________

QUALIFICATIONS & STANDARDS

- Completes Minimum Standard on hardest weeks—system runs without relying on motivation
- Operates diagnostic-first: data before decisions, baselines before solutions
- Governs health information through verified sources—filters influencer noise and unvetted claims
- Pre-plans for predictable disruptions: calendar events are governance opportunities, not surprises
- Applies 24-Hour Rule: single execution miss does not define identity or reset the system
- Sustains sweat equity personally—no outsourcing, no shortcuts, no proxy for the work

47 skills earned. One operating system built.
This role does not end at retirement—it ends when you do.

A Note from the Author

If you have made it this far, thank you. Truly.

In a world full of demands on your time, you chose to spend some of those hours here—building something most people never build. That is not a small thing.

This book started as a simple idea: that the same strategic discipline you apply to running an organization can—and should—be applied to running yourself. Every concept in these pages was built in real life, with real clients, under real pressure. None of it was designed for a controlled environment. All of it was designed for yours.

Your health story is not finished. It is not even close to finished. What you have built here is a system—not a moment. Systems do not expire. They do not require motivation. They require maintenance, honest review, and the willingness to lead.

If something in these pages resonated—a framework that clarified something you already knew, a concept that landed at the right moment, a story that felt familiar—I would be grateful if you shared that in a review. Your voice matters. It reaches people who need this work and have not yet found it.

Whatever part of this journey spoke to you: I am glad you were here for it.

Now lead.

— Adrian M. Williams

About the Author

Adrian M. Williams spent more than two decades as a cybersecurity leader — governing enterprise risk, protecting critical infrastructure, and advising senior leaders on how to build systems that hold under pressure. He has operated across federal, commercial, and nonprofit sectors in environments where the margin for error is measured not in budget but in mission. He holds a Top Secret security clearance and certifications that include C/CISO, PMP, CASP+, CEH, and AWS Solutions Architect.

But the pattern that produced this book did not come from a boardroom. It came from thirty years of 5 a.m. workouts and a lifetime of watching what happens when people treat their health as an afterthought.

The connection Adrian made — early, and clearly — was that the principles governing the most resilient organizations in the world are the same principles that govern a healthy, high-functioning human life. Assess the baseline. Build a system. Remove friction. Review the data. Adjust. Repeat. The framework is identical. The only difference is what most leaders do with it: they apply it at work and abandon themselves at home.

That gap is the reason he became a certified personal trainer alongside his corporate career — and why thirty years of 5 a.m. workouts were never really about fitness. It was always about something harder: building a lifelong operating system for your health — one that survives disruption, does not depend on motivation, and compounds over time the way every good investment does. Over thirty years, hundreds of people came through those early mornings — clients, colleagues, friends, and strangers who showed up looking for a change. What separated those who built something lasting from those who did not was never talent or time. It was always whether they had a system that could survive real life.

Those early mornings — and every conversation that happened in them — are the foundation of every framework in this book.

He consults with organizations and executives as a health strategist — helping leaders apply the same systems discipline they bring to their businesses to the one enterprise they cannot delegate: their own health. He speaks to executive audiences on governance, performance sustainability, and the frameworks that make leadership longevity possible. He lives in the Washington, D.C. area with his wife Tasha.

The CEO of Me: Because Your Health Is Your Business is his first book — and the operating system he has been building toward his entire life.

Notes

Chapter One

1. Centers for Disease Control and Prevention. 'Chronic Diseases in America.' National Center for Chronic Disease Prevention and Health Promotion, 2024. https://www.cdc.gov/chronicdisease

Chapter Two

1. Harrison, Y., and Horne, J.A. 'The Impact of Sleep Deprivation on Decision Making.' Journal of Experimental Psychology: Applied 6, no. 3 (2000): 236–249.

Chapter Three

1. Clear, James. Atomic Habits. New York: Avery, 2018.

2. Walker, Matthew. Why We Sleep. New York: Scribner, 2017.

Chapter Four

1. CDC. 'Chronic Disease Facts.' National Center for Chronic Disease Prevention and Health Promotion, 2021.

2. Baicker, K., Cutler, D., and Song, Z. 'Workplace Wellness Programs Can Generate Savings.' Health Affairs 29, no. 2 (2010): 304–312.

3. Morin, Amy. 'Why LeBron James Sleeps 12 Hours a Day.' Inc. Magazine, 2017.

Chapter Five

1. Colvin, Geoff. 'Mary Barra's Bumpy Ride at GM.' Fortune, 2014.

Chapter Six

1. Middelkamp, J. et al. 'The Effects of Persistence on Exercise Behavior.' Journal of Fitness Research 6, no. 1 (2017).

Chapter Seven

1. Liker, Jeffrey K. The Toyota Way. New York: McGraw-Hill, 2004.

2. Dietary Supplement Health and Education Act of 1994 (DSHEA). Public Law 103-417. U.S. Congress, October 25, 1994.

3. U.S. Senate Committee on Commerce, Science, and Transportation. Hearing on 'Protecting Consumers from False and Deceptive Advertising of Weight-Loss Products.' June 17, 2014. Testimony of Mehmet Oz, M.D.

Chapter Eight

1. Dowd, Maureen. 'Dwayne Johnson, the Most Disciplined Man in Hollywood.' The New York Times, 2019.

2. Saporito, Bill. 'Under Armour's Kevin Plank Is Building a Digital Ecosystem.' Time, 2015.

3. Vary, Adam B. 'Kevin Hart Breaks Down His Recovery.' Variety, 2020.

4. Helm, Burt. 'Domino's Made Itself Over.' Inc. Magazine, 2012.

5. Clear, James. Atomic Habits. New York: Avery, 2018.

Chapter Nine

1. Fothergill, E. et al. 'Persistent Metabolic Adaptation 6 Years After The Biggest Loser Competition.' Obesity 24, no. 8 (2016): 1612–1619.

2. Middelkamp, J. et al. 'The Effects of Persistence on Exercise Behavior.' Journal of Fitness Research 6, no. 1 (2017).